INTERNATIONAL ARBITRATION
A HANDBOOK

THIRD EDITION

CW00345914

DISPUTE RESOLUTION GUIDES

So You Really Want to be an Arbitrator
by D. Mark Cato
(1999)

Introduction to Arbitration
by Harold Crowter
(1998)

Practical Guide to Litigation
Second edition
by Travers Smith Braithwiate
(1998)

What is Dispute Resolution?
by Dr Peter L. d'Ambrumenil
(1998)

INTERNATIONAL ARBITRATION:
A HANDBOOK
THIRD EDITION

PHILLIP CAPPER

Lovells

LLP

LONDON SINGAPORE

2004

Informa Professional
(a trading division of Informa (UK) Ltd)
Mortimer House
37–41 Mortimer Street
London W1T 3JH
professional.enquiries@informa.com

EAST ASIA
Informa Professional
No 1 Grange Road
#08–02 Orchard Building
Singapore
informa.asia@informa.com

First edition 1996
Second edition 1999
Third edition 2004

© Lovells 2004

British Library Cataloguing in Publication Data
A catalogue record for this book
is available from the
British Library

ISBN 1-84311-326-0

Text set in 10/12pt Postscript Plantin by Tony Lansbury, Tonbridge, Kent.
Printed in Great Britain by MPG Books Ltd, Bodmin, Cornwall.

PREFACE TO THE THIRD EDITION

This third edition is much expanded. That is a reflection of the changing face of consensual techniques for the resolution of international disputes. International arbitration is now more frequently used alongside a variety of alternative, or amicable, dispute resolution procedures. We therefore have a new chapter on ADR. There has also been between states a proliferation of foreign investment treaties which use the model of arbitration to allow investors direct remedies. This growing field of bilateral, and multilateral, investment treaty arbitration (BITs and MITs) raises a range of new issues. These also are addressed in a new chapter. BITs and MITs increase the public interest element, which is in tension with the inherently private nature of arbitration. We have therefore reflected in this new edition growing doubts about the confidentiality of international arbitration. Throughout we have sought to update the text. One such important area is the use of information technology in arbitration.

This has been a Lovells team effort. We are greatly indebted to my partners Mark Huleatt-James and Nicholas Gould, who were the authors of the two previous editions. The quality and substance of their work still shines through. The text of this new edition has been prepared by my partners, Andrew Foyle and Mark Huleatt-James, and colleagues, Michael Bignell, Mark Goodrich, Sabine Konrad, Jonathan Leach, Kieron O'Callaghan, Henry Quinlan, John Reynolds, Nick Rudge, Saira Singh and Jeanene Thompson, with further input from my partners, Michael Davison, Roberta Downey, John Gerszt, Robert Hunter, Simon Nesbitt, Patrick Sherrington and, of course, from me. Any errors that remain are entirely mine. I have been greatly assisted in bringing this team effort to a coherent whole by very substantial further work of Saira Singh.

Our aim has remained to further the objectives set for the *Handbook* in its first edition.

25 August 2004   PHILLIP CAPPER

v

PREFACE TO THE SECOND EDITION

The principal changes which have been made to this edition are to take account of the revisions to the arbitration rules of leading international arbitration institutions such as the American Arbitration Association, the China International Economic and Trade Arbitration Commission, the International Court of Arbitration of the International Chamber of Commerce and the London Court of International Arbitration. In addition, where appropriate, small changes have been made to take account of recent cases and statutes, and to enhance the clarity of the text. Alluring as it was, we have resisted the temptation to make significant additions to the detail contained in the book, so as to preserve its role as an introductory text providing an overview of international commercial arbitration.

MARK HULEATT-JAMES

30 September 1998   NICHOLAS GOULD

PREFACE TO THE FIRST EDITION

There are few books dealing with international commercial arbitration generally. Of those that do, none can be described as a slim volume providing an overview of the subject. This presents a problem to those whose objective is to obtain an idea of the most significant aspects of international commercial arbitration, but without being able to devote a considerable amount of time to the task. These people include in-house lawyers with broad responsibilities who have to consider arbitration either as a possible dispute resolution mechanism to be included in an international contract, or as a means of settling an existing or contemplated dispute arising out of an international contract. They need to be primed on issues which are likely to be important without having to read an excessive amount of detail. Equally, busy lawyers in law firms may need to gain a quick overview of the subject, especially if they have previously had little contact with it. Finally, students of the subject may find it helpful to start with an overview of international commercial arbitration which indicates what its principal elements are, and how they relate to each other, before embarking upon a more in-depth study of the subject as a whole.

It is for people such as these that this handbook is intended, and their perceived needs have shaped its scope and content. For that reason, this book cannot be a detailed treatise on the law and practice of international commercial arbitration. If more detail is required, specialist lawyers or text books should be consulted.

MARK HULEATT-JAMES

NICHOLAS GOULD

30 September 1995

CONTENTS

TABLE OF CASES

TABLE OF LEGISLATION

TABLE OF CONVENTIONS, ARBITRATION RULES AND STANDARD CLAUSES

CHAPTER 1

INTRODUCTION

When parties enter into a contract, they should consider, amongst the many other matters of concern to them, how they will resolve any disputes arising out of the contract and how such resolution will be enforced. If the parties are domiciled in the same state, and the contract is to be performed there, then the decision may be simple. They might refer their disputes to the local state court knowing that its judgment will be enforceable against either of them. But if those parties are from different states, or if the contract is to be performed in another state, the decision is more difficult. If the dispute is to be resolved in a state court, then which court in which state, and will that court's judgment be enforceable in other states of interest to one or other of the parties?

A party from one state is usually reluctant to agree that disputes will be referred to the courts of the other party's state. It may have a different legal system or legal culture. There may be concerns about the independence of the judiciary. Quite apart from these considerations, neither party will wish to use a state court if its judgment cannot easily be enforced against the other party.

These issues are not new but they arise more and more frequently. "Globalisation", "international investment", "foreign investment", "international trade" are phrases that are now encountered daily in the Press and other media. That "globalisation" is now a cliché shows how much international trade and investment has grown in recent years. More and more businesses are concerned with international contracts and investment with developed and developing states throughout the world.

Arbitration has, for many centuries, provided an alternative to the courts for the resolution of disputes, both domestically and internationally. However, in the last half century international arbitration has developed to the point at which it now provides a well established mechanism for resolving disputes internationally. It is a mechanism which is recognised and supported by the laws of most developed and developing nations. Indeed many states encourage the resolution of disputes by arbitration instead of through the state courts.

The aim of this book is to provide an introduction to, and overview of, international commercial arbitration for those involved with arbitration when negotiating contracts or dealing with disputes, or for those interested as part of their wider studies. The book also explains how arbitration can now be used

1

to enforce the rights and protections offered by multilateral and bilateral investment treaties.

The intention is to provide enough to give a sufficient understanding of the subject without descending to the detail. The book identifies issues which may require more detailed consideration. In such cases reference should be made to the many in depth texts on arbitration.

In this introductory chapter, we describe what arbitration is, its essential characteristics and how it differs from other forms of dispute resolution. We describe the basic legal infrastructure of international arbitration and the role that state courts play in support of arbitration. We explain why parties to commercial contracts might wish to choose arbitration to settle their disputes and the factors to be considered when making that choice.

The intention is that this book may be read from beginning to end to provide an overall understanding of international commercial arbitration. Readers who have a general familiarity with arbitration may simply refer to the chapters which deal with the specific topic of interest.

What is arbitration and how does it differ from other forms of dispute resolution?

Arbitration may be described in general terms as a consensual, private process for the submission of a dispute for a decision of a tribunal, comprising one or more independent third persons. In making its decision, the tribunal must follow certain basic requirements, such as to act fairly and impartially, allowing each party to put its case and to respond to that of its opponent. The decision of the tribunal (referred to as the award) is final and legally binding on the parties and will be recognised and enforced by the courts of most states around the world.

Arbitration differs from court proceedings in that:

(a) arbitration is a consensual process; a party cannot be compelled to arbitrate a dispute unless it has agreed to arbitration;

(b) arbitration is a private and, under many systems of law, confidential process;

(c) in arbitration the parties have the power and freedom to:
   (i) select the tribunal (or agree the method of selection) and can therefore appoint a tribunal with the qualifications and experience to decide the dispute;
   (ii) choose the rules that will apply to the proceedings; and
   (iii) choose the language of the arbitration.

In addition to court and arbitration proceedings, there are many alternative dispute resolution processes, referred to collectively by the acronym "ADR". These alternative methods are described in Chapter 4. They all involve the use of a neutral third person (or persons) to assist in the resolution of the dispute. These ADR processes may be divided into those which require the third person to make a binding decision (such as expert determination) and those which do not, such as mediation.

Unlike arbitration and court proceedings, none of these ADR methods requires the third person to apply due process in reaching the decision (other than Adjudication in construction contracts, at least to some degree) and none result in a decision enforceable like a court judgment or arbitration award.

The legal infrastructure of international arbitration

If international arbitration were a physical structure, its two main foundations would be:

(a) the New York Convention on the Recognition and Enforcement of Foreign Arbitral Awards of 1958 ("the New York Convention"), and

(b) the United Nations Commission for International Trade Law ("UNCITRAL") Model Law on International Commercial Arbitration ("the UNCITRAL Model Law") and the UNCITRAL Arbitration Rules.

Its superstructure would consist of the laws of the states where arbitrations are conducted; together with the rules and practices of the leading international arbitral institutions. Such institutions include the International Court of Arbitration of the International Chamber of Commerce ("ICC"), the LCIA (formerly known as the London Court of International Arbitration) and the International Centre for Dispute Resolution ("ICDR"), the international division of the American Arbitration Association ("AAA").

The New York Convention was a landmark in the development of international arbitration. It requires contracting states to enforce valid arbitration agreements and introduced a straightforward procedure for obtaining the recognition or enforcement of arbitral awards internationally. The Convention has been ratified by over 130 states, thus providing the most extensive network for the enforcement of decisions resolving disputes. The regime established by the New York Convention for the enforcement of arbitration awards far exceeds any comparable international regime for enforcing court decisions.

The New York Convention defines the specific grounds upon which recognition and enforcement of an arbitration award may be refused by a state court. One of these grounds is that the party against whom the award is invoked was not given proper notice of the appointment of the arbitrator or of the arbitration proceedings or was otherwise unable to present its case.

The New York Convention does not prescribe how an arbitration is to be conducted, but by listing the grounds upon which enforcement may be refused, it effectively defines the basic requirements and establishes a benchmark.

In Chapter 2 of this book we identify the applicable laws and rules that are relevant to arbitration and which must be observed by a tribunal to ensure that its award will be recognised and enforced. As there explained, the arbitration must be conducted in accordance with the relevant state's arbitration law applying to the proceedings and in accordance with the rules that the parties have agreed will apply to the proceedings.

In the last 30 years, significant steps have been taken to ensure that states throughout the world have arbitration laws which satisfy the basic requirements of a modern arbitration law. UNCITRAL has led the way by promulgating its Model Law on arbitration and its Arbitration Rules. Extensive reference is made to the UNCITRAL Model Law and Arbitration Rules throughout this book and they are described in more detail in Chapter 2. The intention of the Model Law is to provide a precedent for those states that wish to introduce a modern arbitration law. To date, 42 states have adopted the Model Law, in whole or in part, as the basis for their national law of arbitration. Many more have based their arbitration law on the Model Law.

Finally, the legal superstructure of international arbitration includes the rules and practices of the leading arbitral institutions. Partly as a result of the activities of these arbitral institutions, supplemented by the activities of academic institutions, there is a growing body of international law and practice relating to international arbitration which is documented in the many legal journals and texts relating to arbitration. There is also a growing community of lawyers and other professionals who practise arbitration law, either by representing parties in arbitrations or by appointments as arbitrators, and who contribute to the growing culture of international arbitration.

The significance of the labels "international" and "commercial"

This book is about those arbitrations which may be characterised as "international" and "commercial". This characterisation has significant legal implications and practical consequences.

Legal significance – "international" character

The starting point is that the New York Convention applies to the enforcement of awards not considered as domestic awards in the state where their recognition and enforcement is sought. The New York Convention therefore recognises that a different legal regime may apply to domestic awards.

A number of states, such as France, Italy, Singapore and Switzerland, impose different legal requirements on domestic arbitrations. It is always necessary to check the relevant state's arbitration law for the definition of "international arbitration". Usually this will be the law of the state in which the arbitration is to take place.

In this book the definition in the UNCITRAL Model Law has been adopted. International arbitrations are those:
(a) which involve parties which have their places of business in different states, or
(b) which deal with disputes

    (i) arising out of obligations to be performed, or

    (ii) connected with subject-matter

in a different state from the place of business of at least one of the parties.

The international nature of arbitration has a number of practical consequences. For at least one party (and some or all of the members of the tribunal) at least one foreign state and one foreign legal system will be involved. Dealing with a dispute which involves a foreign element, possibly in a foreign territory, is logistically more complicated and expensive than dealing with a domestic dispute. However, the location of the arbitration and the law that will apply to the contract are matters which may be agreed between the parties.

"Commercial" nature

Some states also treat commercial arbitrations differently from non-commercial disputes. This distinction is reflected in the New York Convention which provides that a state acceding to the Convention may declare that it will apply the Convention only to differences arising out of legal relationships, whether contractual or not, which are considered as commercial under the national law of the state making such declaration. A large number of states have availed themselves of this reservation. Appendix 1 contains a list of the signatory states to this Convention and indicates those which rely on the "commercial reservation".

The New York Convention recognises that the definition of "commercial" is left to the national law of the relevant state. There is no uniform definition and some states' arbitration laws adopt unusual definitions. For example, at the time of writing, Vietnam does not include construction disputes in its definition of commercial disputes, although it is understood that the definition is to be widened to include construction disputes.

The UNCITRAL Model Law applies to "international commercial arbitration" but does not define "commercial". However, a guidance note suggests that "the term 'commercial' should be given a wide interpretation so as to cover matters arising from all relationships of a commercial nature, whether contractual or not" (note to Article 1(1)).

This book is concerned with international commercial arbitration. It does not cover arbitration involving consumers. In any event, international arbitration is unlikely to be appropriate for consumer contracts. In a 1998 case (*Brower* v. *Gateway 2000*), the New York Supreme Court struck out part of an arbitration agreement purporting to refer disputes arising under a consumer contract to ICC arbitration, requiring the ICC to be substituted (presumably by a more appropriate domestic organisation).

The role of state courts in relation to arbitration

International arbitrations do not occur within a legal vacuum. Every arbitration has a legal foundation, or juridical "seat", in one country. An arbitration must be conducted in accordance with the arbitration law of that state. However, most modern state arbitration laws, particularly those which follow the Model Law, recognise and apply two basic principles. First, that the parties should be free to agree how their disputes are resolved, subject only to certain basic safeguards. Second, that the state courts should intervene in the arbitral process as little as possible.

Although the state courts should not intervene in the arbitral process, such courts have an important role in supporting arbitration and are frequently called upon to do so. For example, the courts of most states with modern arbitration laws will:

(a) recognise a valid arbitration agreement and will stay (i.e. prevent from going forward) any state court proceedings brought in contravention of that arbitration agreement (indeed, the New York Convention requires states to recognise arbitration agreements and to refer, at the request of one of the parties, a dispute to arbitration unless the court concludes that the arbitration agreement is null and void, inoperative or incapable of being performed);

(b) assist in the appointment or removal of an arbitrator;

(c) issue interim orders to protect the subject matter of the dispute;

(d) assist in the enforcement of an arbitral award.

In none of these examples does the state court make a final decision on the merits of the dispute. However, courts do have powers to review or set aside the award or to refuse enforcement of the award. An unsuccessful party may challenge an award (i.e. attack its validity or effect) in the courts of the juridical seat of the arbitration or in the courts of the state where enforcement is sought.

The extent to which a state court may review or set aside an award will depend on the law of the state in question. Recognition and enforcement of awards and resisting awards are dealt with in detail in Chapters 9 and 10 of this book. It is sufficient in this Introduction to note only that the arbitration laws of either the juridical seat of the arbitration or the state in which enforcement of an award is sought will permit the state courts to set aside an award or refuse enforcement on limited grounds.

The New York Convention provides that recognition and enforcement of an arbitration award may only be refused, at the request of the party against whom it is invoked, on certain specified grounds (Article V). These grounds include the following:

(a) the party against whom the award is invoked was not given proper notice of the appointment of the arbitrator or of the arbitration proceedings or was otherwise unable to present his case; or

(b) the award deals with a difference not contemplated by or not falling within the terms of the submission to arbitration, or it contains decisions on matters beyond the scope of the submission to arbitration.

The arbitration laws of states which are signatories to the New York Convention should reflect its provisions.

States whose arbitration laws adopt the UNCITRAL Model Law on arbitration will limit the grounds on which the courts of the juridical seat can set aside an award to the same grounds as are specified in the New York Convention for resisting enforcement of an award.

Some states' arbitration laws give the courts of the juridical seat wider powers to review awards. Some arbitration laws even permit the unsuccessful party to challenge the award on points of law. In such cases, it is often permissible for the parties to agree to exclude the right to appeal to the courts.

Choosing between arbitration and court proceedings

The parties to international commercial contracts have the power and freedom to select the means by which their disputes will be resolved. Usually this choice is made at the contracting stage. Even if the parties did not include an arbitration agreement in their original contract, it is still possible for them to agree that an existing dispute will be referred to arbitration. A few states around the world still require that the agreement to arbitrate be made only after the dispute has arisen.

The choice of the dispute resolution method will always depend on the circumstances of each case. For some types of contract, e.g. engineering and construction contracts, arbitration is the dispute resolution method widely preferred by the industry. For other contracts, such as loan agreements, arbitration remains much less common because lenders may consider that arbitration is not the quickest and simplest method to enforce the obligation of the borrower to repay the loan, or the simplest method to enforce the lender's security.

Key factors to be considered when choosing the dispute resolution forum include: the type of dispute that might arise out of the contract, the identity and nationality of the parties, the courts which might otherwise have jurisdiction and the location of assets of the parties.

It is possible for parties to a contract to agree that certain disputes arising under the contract are to be submitted to arbitration, whilst others are to be settled by state courts. In such a case, the jurisdictions of the courts and the arbitration remain exclusive for the particular dispute which has been referred to them. Unless these agreements are carefully drafted there can be disputes as to the extent of the jurisdiction of the arbitration or the courts.

In general terms, arbitration may be appropriate in the following circumstances:

(a) The parties cannot agree which state court will have jurisdiction to determine disputes. There will be many reasons why one party may be reluctant to accept the state court of the other party, including distrust of the degree of judicial independence and unsatisfactory court procedures. The procedures of some state courts are still cumbersome and lengthy or may have unattractive features for some parties.

(b) The enforceability of the judgment or award is a critical factor. How and where will any state court decision or arbitration award be enforced? If one of the parties does not have any assets in the territory of the state court, then referring disputes to that court will make no commercial sense if its judgment will not be recognised and enforced in a different state where the party does have assets.

(c) The chosen governing law of the parties' principal contract may be different from the law of the state, or states where the parties are domiciled. While many state courts are experienced in applying a foreign law, others are not. Furthermore, the procedures for proving a foreign law may be very different in some state courts.

(d) The language of the contract may be different from the language of the state court of one or more of the parties. The parties may not wish to add to the logistical problems of dealing with the dispute by requiring all documents to be translated into that state's language.

(e) The parties may wish to have a final binding decision which is not subject to an appeal. In many states, it is not possible to appeal against an arbitration award on the grounds that the arbitrator made an error of law. In other states it is possible for the parties to agree to exclude the right of appeal on points of law. For some parties this element of finality is desirable.

Earlier in this chapter, some of the main differences between arbitration and state court proceedings were identified. If parties wish to take advantage of some of those differences (such as privacy, and the freedom to select the tribunal and the procedure) then they will prefer arbitration to resolve their dispute.

Arbitration may be neither appropriate nor possible in the following circumstances, for example:

(a) The dispute is not "arbitrable" under the law applicable to the arbitration agreement itself, the law of the state where it is intended that the arbitration should take place, or the law of the state where the award is to be enforced. (The "arbitrability" of disputes is discussed at page 13 below.)

(b) One of the intended parties lacks the capacity, under the law of its domicile, to participate in an arbitration (see page 12 below). For example, the Saudi Arabian state may not be a party to an arbitration agreement. The US federal government cannot be a party, though state agencies may be. There are other states, such as Iran, that can only be parties to an arbitration agreement when there has been a specific authorisation given by the relevant state authority.

(c) The nature of the remedy likely to be sought in the proceedings is not normally within the powers of an arbitral tribunal: for example, if the party is likely to be seeking a coercive order, such as a permanent injunction.

(d) Quicker and cheaper proceedings may be available in some states' courts – for example, summary judgment on liquidated debts.

(e) There are multi-party problems because the proceedings involve more than two parties and involve disputes arising out of related contracts (see pages 38–46 below).

In some circumstances arbitration may be more expensive than state court proceedings. The parties to arbitration must pay the fees of the arbitrator and the costs of the arbitration venue, as well as the administrative fees of any arbitral institution, such as the ICC, which may be involved. In most states, the courts, though not a free service, are comparatively cheap.

Making arbitration work

"Party autonomy" is a fundamental principle of international arbitration. It means the freedom of parties to agree how their disputes are to be resolved, subject only to certain basic safeguards. Parties are free to decide not only whether, but also how, their disputes should be arbitrated. Making these decisions is not, however, a simple matter. There are potentially complicated issues to be considered. For example, unlike the context in domestic contracts, in the context of international arbitration it is necessary to consider a number of different systems of law and the interaction of those laws with the provisions of the proposed arbitration agreement and arbitral rules.

We hope this book will dispel two common misconceptions. First, many who negotiate contracts believe that the arbitration clause is a straightforward provision to be added to the end of the agreement, with little thought as to its implications and consequences. This book is intended to identify the main issues and factors to be considered at the contract drafting stage.

Secondly, those involved with disputes often believe that the arbitration procedure should simply mimic the state court procedures with which that person is most familiar. To make that mistake is to forego the many benefits that arbitration can provide and may indeed make the arbitration proceedings unworkable.

To paraphrase one modern state arbitration law, the object of arbitration is to obtain the fair resolution of disputes by an impartial tribunal without unnecessary delay or expense. To this end the tribunal should adopt procedures suitable to the circumstances of the particular case. These principles are reflected in many other state arbitration laws and in the rules of the leading international arbitral institutions.

It is our hope that this book will help those who are involved with disputes to maximise the advantages of international arbitration.

CHAPTER 2

APPLICABLE LAWS AND RULES

INTRODUCTION

This chapter will focus on three related areas which establish a framework within which an international commercial arbitration can take place: first, the various applicable laws which may need to be considered in the context of an international commercial arbitration; secondly, the international conventions and treaties that are relevant to international commercial arbitration; and thirdly, the UNCITRAL Model Law and Arbitration Rules, which represent an attempt to promote greater uniformity in international commercial arbitration.

APPLICABLE LAWS

A number of systems of law may simultaneously have some application to an international commercial arbitration. For example, take the case of a Delaware corporation having a contract with a Tunisian corporation which is expressed to be governed by English law. The contract provides that any disputes arising out of it are to be submitted to arbitration in Paris pursuant to the Arbitration Rules of the ICC. It is immediately apparent that a number of systems of law may be relevant in the case. These will include, amongst others, the law applicable to:

(a) determine the capacity of a party to enter into the arbitration agreement;
(b) the arbitration agreement itself;
(c) the arbitration proceedings (often referred to as the "lex arbitri"), i.e. the law of the seat of the arbitration;
(d) the dispute itself (the "lex causae"); and,
(e) the enforcement of any award.

A party to a potential dispute can properly consider its position only when it knows which law, or laws, may be applicable. There is no complete code, for determining applicable law, which has general international application. The legal system of each state has its own particular approach and, if clarification of that approach is required, advice from lawyers in the relevant state will have to be obtained. What is set out below can be no more than a brief summary of approaches which have some measure of general acceptance. Furthermore, as we shall see below, in an international arbitration the determination of what law is applicable, e.g. to the dispute itself, may not be dependent on the way in which any particular state court would approach that question.

Capacity

In the case of corporate or state entities, the law applicable to establish capacity to enter into an arbitration agreement (or to continue with proceedings in the event of insolvency) will usually be the law of the state in which the entity has its domicile. The fact that corporations have power to enter into arbitration agreements by the law of the place of an arbitration will not generally be enough to give a corporation such a power if it lacks it in the state in which it is domiciled. A lack of capacity to arbitrate will be fatal to the enforcement of any award which may be made (see page 131 below).

The arbitration agreement

Though an arbitration agreement is often encountered as just one of a number of clauses in a written contract, it is accepted by the arbitration laws of very many states that the arbitration agreement is to be treated as a separate agreement and that the arbitration agreement does not automatically terminate when the contract of which its is part comes to an end. This is the so-called concept of the "autonomy", "separability" or "severability" of the arbitration agreement, the practical significance of which is dealt with at page 81. It follows that the law applicable to an arbitration agreement can be different from that applicable to the principal contract between the parties. This may arise from express agreement between the parties or by operation of law.

Arbitration agreements are specifically excluded from the application of the rules of the Rome Convention on the Law Applicable to Contractual Obligations of 1980. (The European Commission's Green Paper of January 2003 on the conversion of the Rome Convention into a Community Instrument and its modernisation proposes that such exclusion should be continued.) However, the basis on which to determine the applicable law of the arbitration agreement may well be the same as those for establishing the applicable law of the principal contract itself. These are dealt with below under the heading "The dispute".

Arbitration derogates from the state's ability to intervene in the resolution of disputes which may involve one of its nationals or domiciliaries. When this simply involves day-to-day commercial transactions, that may not be of much concern to the state. However, when it involves matters such as the welfare of individuals (for example, when financial provision for the family on the break-up of a marriage is at issue), rights of third parties in an insolvency, competition issues, intellectual property rights and certain aspects of employment disputes, the state may well wish to intervene or to reserve to itself the powers of control and resolution, as a matter of public policy.

This leads on to the concept of the "arbitrability" of disputes. A dispute which is not "arbitrable" under the law applicable to the arbitration agreement cannot be settled by arbitration. The same is true for a dispute which is not arbitrable under the *lex arbitri*, i.e. the arbitration law of the seat. An award made in respect of any such disputes, or a dispute which is not arbitrable under the law of the state in which enforcement of the award is sought, will not be enforceable in such state (see Article V(1)(a) and (2)(a) of the New York Convention).

The arbitrability of a dispute is therefore an important issue and one to which attention should be given in relation to each of the three principal stages of an arbitration, i.e. when:

(a) the arbitration agreement is being made;
(b) the arbitration is commenced; and
(c) the enforcement of an award is sought.

The arbitration proceedings

There has been a trend, especially in certain states in continental Europe, to treat international commercial arbitration as a means of dispute resolution to be completely independent of any form of state control, except at the stage of the enforcement of an award. In other words, the courts of the state in which an arbitration is taking place are not to interfere with the arbitration and, in particular, that they should not interfere with the procedure under which the arbitration is conducted or with any decisions made by the arbitrator. Such a trend has variously been described, such as for example as the "delocalisation" theory of international commercial arbitration.

It is beyond the scope of a book such as this to consider delocalisation theory in detail. It was conceived, in large part, to deal with the difficulty of reconciling the immunity of states involved in arbitration proceedings with control of those proceedings by the courts of the other state in which they take place. It is now said to apply to international commercial arbitrations, whether or not they involve a state party. Its proponents point out that the state in which an arbitration takes place is often selected for a wide variety of reasons and that it is inappropriate that that the laws of that state should have any bearing on the conduct of the arbitration. All that should be required is compliance with the norms of international public policy.

This theory does not have general acceptance, particularly in countries with legal systems based on the common law. It may however be encountered in practice often when a state, or a state entity, is involved in the arbitration.

The more widely accepted (and, it is submitted, correct) view is that arbitrations cannot be conducted in a legal vacuum. There may be occasions when it may be necessary to:

(a) appoint an arbitrator, if the parties to the arbitration cannot agree on the appointment;

(b) remove and replace an arbitrator for bias, or other misconduct;

(c) provide assistance to arbitrators (e.g. by enforcing attendance by witnesses at a hearing);

(d) establish whether an award is valid and final.

The performance of these functions clearly cannot be left entirely to the arbitrators and the parties. An obvious mechanism for their performance is a court of the state (the "seat") in which the arbitration is taking place – it alone has the power to enforce its decisions in that country. In accepting jurisdiction and reaching its decisions, such a court will apply its own law. One thus arrives at the "seat" theory, which is that the law applicable to the arbitration proceedings is that of the state in which they take place (i.e. are juridically rooted, even if meetings or hearings are actually conducted for convenience elsewhere).

Whilst it is quite possible for parties to choose, by agreement, a procedural law applicable to the arbitration proceedings which is not the same as the arbitration law of the "seat"' of the arbitration, it is not easy to envisage circumstances in which it would be suitable to do so (save in the special case of arbitrations coming into existence pursuant to an international treaty, such as ICSID arbitrations – see further, Chapter 11 on investment treaty arbitration).

Save where the parties have agreed otherwise, the failure of the arbitral procedure to comply with the arbitration law of the state which is the seat of the arbitration will render the award unenforceable (see Article V(1)(d) of the New York Convention).

The dispute

The determination of the law applicable to the arbitration itself (as opposed to the substance of the disputes) is based on what are essentially practical considerations. However, different tests must be applied to determine what should be the law applicable to the dispute between the parties (the *lex causae* referred to on page 11).

For example, a Russian party may be in dispute with an English one over the value of minerals to be delivered to Germany. It may have submitted that dispute to arbitration which takes place in France. Russian, English and German law each have some connection with the dispute, but none is obviously "practical" – at least one of the parties, and possibly the arbitral tribunal, will have to deal with a legal system with which it has little or no familiarity.

How is the law applicable to the substance of dispute to be determined? State courts, to whose jurisdiction litigants are obliged to submit (because of the domicile of the defendant, or some connection with the subject-matter of the dispute, or prior agreement) have established their own rules for making that determination. Except where they have been harmonised by a convention such as the Rome Convention of 1980, the rules will differ from state to state. Where, however, an international dispute has been submitted to arbitration, it will often be the case that the parties will have reached no agreement as to the seat of the arbitration and the arbitrator (or an institution such as the ICC, if it has been appointed) will have to make a decision on that question. The seat of the arbitration may turn out to be in the state which is physically the most convenient for the parties and the arbitral tribunal. There is no obvious reason why the rules of that state (the seat) for determining the law applicable to the dispute should be used. Furthermore, the arbitral tribunal is not linked to that state in the same way as a judge in its courts is.

The most important principle (a principle which is widely accepted and fundamental in international arbitration) is that of party autonomy, which as explained on page 9 is the freedom of the parties to choose what they want for their arbitration. In the context of the determination of the law applicable to the substance of the dispute, this has two facets:

(a) The parties may choose the law which is to apply to their dispute (so long as the choice is *bona fide* and legal); or

(b) failing such a choice, the parties may establish how the arbitral tribunal is to choose the applicable law. Thus, if the parties have decided that the ICC Arbitration Rules are to apply, Article 17(1) of those rules provides that the "Arbitral Tribunal shall apply the rules of law which it determines to be appropriate". Article 33(1) of the UNCITRAL Arbitration Rules contains a very similar provision. In practice, in making their choice, arbitrators tend (subject to what is said in the next paragraph) to look to what they regard as general principles of conflicts of laws, or the conflict of law system of the seat of the arbitration, or to some other system which they consider has a connection with the dispute.

Where nothing has been agreed between the parties as to the law applicable to the dispute, or as to how it is to be determined, care has to be exercised. Some countries, such as France, the Netherlands and Switzerland, have in their laws applicable to international commercial arbitrations a provision that the arbitral tribunal is able to decide for itself what rules it considers are appropriate to settle the dispute. Many other countries do not have such a liberal arbitration regime and require the arbitral tribunal to apply the conflict of laws rules of the seat of the arbitration.

Another important matter to bear in mind is the nature of the law which is applicable to an international commercial contract. Because the parties may come from very different legal backgrounds they may find it difficult to come to a compromise as to the system of law which is to govern the contract between them. Often, where one of the parties is a state and that party insists on the application to the contract of its own system of law, the other party will wish to protect its position against future changes in that law. This it may achieve by obtaining agreement to the application to the contract of principles of international law (such as the obligation to pay appropriate compensation following an act of nationalisation) as a "concurrent" law (i.e. a law whose general principles will operate alongside, and control, the application of the state's system of law). Such a party may also seek the state's agreement to a "stabilisation clause" – that is, a provision in the contract to the effect that the state will not rely on changes in its law to deprive the other party of its benefits under the contract, or that if it does, it will pay compensation. (The efficacy of such clauses is, however, open to doubt because it is not clear that states may bind their freedom of legislative action in this way.)

Where the parties are on a more equal commercial footing, they may adopt other techniques to arrive at a law applicable to disputes which will be acceptable to both of them. One such technique is to make the contract subject to the *lex mercatoria* or international trade law – i.e. to those principles governing the conduct of international trade which are generally accepted by international traders. This technique suffers from the deficiency that there is no clear statement available as to what these principles are.

Another technique which is frequently encountered in practice is to supplement the applicable state law by requiring the arbitral tribunal to take into account relevant "trade usages" (which would include generally accepted meanings for terms which are in common use in contracts made in the relevant trade). The laws of a number of countries permit or require this in any event. The ICC Arbitration Rules (Article 17(2)) and the UNCITRAL Arbitration Rules (Article 33(3)) require it.

Finally, in the context of the law applicable to the substance of the dispute, one may also consider the power of "amiable composition", or the power of an arbitral tribunal to decide "*ex aequo et bono*". As with much of the practice relating to international commercial arbitration, there is no precise and generally accepted definition of what these are. A useful approximation is that they permit an arbitral tribunal, in the course of making an enforceable award, to arrive at a decision which it thinks is fair, even if it is not strictly in accordance with the applicable law. An arbitral tribunal may only make use of these powers if the parties have agreed that it can do so. If such powers are to be conferred on an arbitral tribunal it may be best to choose arbitrators more for their knowledge of the subject-matter of the dispute between the parties than for their knowledge of the applicable law. Such powers may also be conferred on an arbitral tribunal when the parties have entered into a long-term agreement and are anxious that disputes arising during the currency of the agreement should be resolved without harming the continuing relationship between them.

Recognition or enforcement of awards

The law which is applicable to the recognition or enforcement of an award is that of the state in which enforcement is sought (e.g. where the debtor's assets are located). That law will determine not only the procedure to be adopted for applications for recognition or enforcement, but also the defences to any such applications. For these purposes many states have incorporated into their laws the provisions of the New York Convention.

It is important to note that systems of law other than that of the place of enforcement may become relevant. Article V(1) of the New York Convention provides that recognition and enforcement may be refused, among other grounds, where:

   (a) the parties to the arbitration agreement were, under the law applicable to them, under some incapacity;

   (b) the arbitration agreement is not valid under the applicable law agreed upon by the parties or, failing any indication as to that, under the law of the country where the award was made;

   (c) the composition of the arbitral tribunal, or the arbitral procedure used, was not in accordance with the agreement of the parties, or, failing agreement, was not in accordance with the law of the state where the arbitration took place (the seat).

INTERNATIONAL CONVENTIONS AND TREATIES

The reference to the New York Convention leads into the important topic of the conventions which are relevant to international commercial arbitration. The most important conventions are the multilateral conventions (i.e. entered into between three or more states) designed to ensure the international enforceability of arbitration agreements and awards and which become incorporated into the law of the contracting states to such conventions.

The Geneva Protocol of 1923

The first significant international convention was the Geneva Protocol of 1923, prepared under the auspices of the League of Nations. Its primary objective was to secure the international enforcement of arbitration agreements. It was also intended to ensure that arbitration awards would be enforced in the states in which they were made.

The Geneva Convention of 1927

The principal purpose of the Geneva Convention was to extend the scope of the Geneva Protocol so that an award made in one contracting state would be enforced in any of the other contracting states, and not only in the state in which it was made.

The New York Convention of 1958

One of the major drawbacks of the Geneva Protocol and Convention was that they put the onus on the party seeking enforcement to prove that the conditions required for enforcement had been fulfilled. This could be burdensome. It sometimes required making an application to the courts of the state in which the award was made and it was not effective to promote the use of arbitration as an efficient means of settling international commercial disputes. The New York Convention, drawn up under the auspices of the United Nations, has changed that, becoming in the process the most important international convention relating to international commercial arbitration.

The New York Convention replaces the Geneva Protocol and Convention for all states. It requires contracting states to enforce valid arbitration agreements (discussed in more detail at pages 25 *et seq.* below), it has introduced a much more straightforward procedure for obtaining the recognition or enforcement of arbitral awards (as to which, see page 125 below) and it reverses the burden of the Geneva Protocol and Convention by placing the principal burden on the party resisting recognition or enforcement of an award to establish the reasons why the award should not be recognised or enforced.

The significance of the New York Convention cannot be overemphasised. As already mentioned in Chapter 1, it has been ratified by over 130 states around the world, thus providing the most extensive network presently in existence for the enforcement of decisions resolving disputes (see Appendix 1 for a list of the contracting states).

The European Convention on International Commercial Arbitration of 1961

One of the main purposes of this convention was to facilitate East–West trade, though it was open for signature by states which were not European. Unlike the New York Convention, the European Convention only applies when the parties to the arbitration reside in contracting states. The European Convention has been ratified by only 26 states and lacks the significance of the New York Convention.

The Washington Convention of 1965

This convention provides for the establishment of the International Centre for the Settlement of Investment Disputes (ICSID). It is often referred to as "the ICSID Convention". ICSID arbitration is designed to deal with disputes arising out of investments made in a contracting state (under an agreement with the state itself, or a designated state agency) by a national of another contracting state. The Washington Convention is important because, at the time of writing, 140 states have ratified it and provision for ICSID arbitration is included in a large number of international contracts. The Washington Convention was sponsored by the World Bank, and the authority of the bank may be available to assist in the enforcement of an ICSID award.

The subject of investment treaty arbitration is discussed in some detail in Chapter 11.

The Moscow Convention of 1972

The Moscow Convention was concluded as part of the process for the implementation of the "socialist economic integration" of the countries belonging to the Council of Mutual Economic Assistance (CMEA). It required "economic organisations" in the states which were parties to the Convention to resolve their disputes by arbitration by the courts of arbitration at designated chambers of commerce in such states. It gave awards made in such arbitration the same effect as final judgments and made provision for their reciprocal enforcement.

With the break-up of the CMEA, the status of the Moscow Convention has been thrown into doubt. It has been denounced by a number of the states which were a party to it and others are considering denunciation. It has, in effect, become largely obsolete.

The Panama Convention of 1975

Latin American countries had to a degree mistrusted US and European business interests, and the arbitration organisations regarded as under the latter's influence, though Latin America has come to recognise the benefits of international arbitration. These states were slow to ratify the New York Convention, preferring their own convention, the Panama Convention, which nevertheless adopts many of the principles of the New York Convention. There are two particularly significant aspects of the Panama Convention. First, it does not contain provision for the enforcement of arbitration agreements. Secondly, if the parties fail to agree upon the procedure for the arbitration, the Inter-American Commercial Arbitration Commission (IACAC) Rules of Procedure will apply. These are now the UNCITRAL Arbitration Rules (see page 21).

The OHADA Treaty of 1993

OHADA is the French acronym for the Organisation for the Harmonisation of Business Law in Africa. The OHADA Treaty was signed by 16 Francophone African countries (the Treaty is also open for signature by the countries which are members of the Organisation for African Unity) in 1993. Its main objectives include the modernisation and harmonisation of business law in Africa in order to re-establish investor confidence and to facilitate trade between the contracting states and the promotion of arbitration to settle commercial disputes.

Arbitration proceedings which are conducted in the OHADA area are governed by:

(a) the OHADA Treaty, which establishes the constitutional framework and confirms the enforcement of arbitration agreements;
(b) the Uniform Arbitration Act, which sets out the law applicable to arbitrations conducted in the OHADA signatory states (and is in some respects similar to the UNCITRAL Model Law);
(c) the Arbitration Rules of the Common Court of Justice and Arbitration (which have much in common with the ICC Arbitration Rules) which set out the procedures pursuant to which the arbitration is to be conducted.

The North American Free Trade Agreement of 1994 (NAFTA)

The NAFTA was signed by Canada, the United States and Mexico in 1992 and came into force on 1 January 1994. It was established to promote, amongst other things, free trade and the protection and enforcement of rights among its signatory countries based on the principles of non-discrimination, transparency, co-operation and due process.

The NAFTA provides a mechanism for the settlement of disputes arising out of investments between a NAFTA party and an investor of another NAFTA party that assures both equal treatment among investors of the NAFTA parties in accordance with the principle of international reciprocity and due process before an impartial tribunal. Private parties who have a dispute with a NAFTA party other than their own state may commence an arbitration which will be subject to one of three applicable sets of arbitration rules. These are the ICSID Arbitration Rules (see page 18 above and Chapter 11), the Additional Facility Rules of ICSID (where one of the disputing parties is not a party to the ICSID Convention) (see Chapter 11) or the UNCITRAL Arbitration Rules (see below).

Bilateral treaties

These are treaties made between two states. Whilst multilateral conventions are of great significance for international commercial arbitration as a whole, that fact should not obscure the usefulness of bilateral treaties, particularly where the dispute involves a party or, more importantly, a party which has an asset, not located in a contracting state to the New York Convention. The claimant may be reluctant to commence an arbitration in the respondent's home state, fearing judicial interference. In such a case it should attempt to obtain agreement to the place of the arbitration being in a state which has a bilateral convention for the enforcement of arbitral awards with the country in which the respondent's asset is located. Better still, the state in which the arbitration is to take place should also be a contracting state to the New York Convention so that any award made can also be enforced against any other assets of the respondent which may be found in other contracting states to the New York Convention. Bilateral investment treaties also confer useful advantages (see page 136 below).

THE UNCITRAL ARBITRATION RULES AND MODEL LAW

International commercial arbitration suffers from a lack of uniformity in the laws applicable to it. In the general commercial field attempts are being made to create greater uniformity in the laws applicable to the substance of the relationship between the parties to an agreement (e.g. the Vienna Convention on Contracts for the International Sale of Goods of 1980 – also promoted by UNCITRAL). In addition, the Rome Convention of 1980 (see page 12 above) attempts to harmonise the rules for determining the law which will be applicable to a contractual relationship.

However, in the case of the laws applicable to the arbitration proceedings themselves, there was and, to a lesser extent, remains a substantial problem in that some states (particularly in the developing world) scarcely have any system of arbitration law at all. In addition, guidance was lacking as to the nature of the rules which should be adopted in arbitrations not subject to the rules of institutions such as the ICC and the LCIA. Compliance with a set of rules is important if awards made in such arbitrations are to be enforceable.

The UNCITRAL Arbitration Rules

The UNCITRAL Arbitration Rules were prepared in consultation with lawyers from many states and were published in final form in 1976. The key points about these rules are the following:

(a) The UNICITRAL Rules were designed for use in "*ad hoc*" or "non-institutional" arbitrations, i.e. those arbitrations in which the parties, alone or with the arbitral tribunal, devise and administer their own procedures, as opposed to "institutional" arbitrations, which are administered by an arbitral institution and conducted in accordance with the arbitration rules of such an institution (e.g. the ICC, the LCIA or the AAA/ICDR as to which see page 31). (Some institutions, such as the LCIA and the AAA/ICDR, are prepared to administer arbitrations which are conducted in accordance with the UNCITRAL Arbitration Rules, rather than their own rules, if the parties so agree.) Arbitral institutions are also generally willing to act simply as appointing authorities, to appoint an arbitrator for an arbitration which is otherwise *ad hoc*.

(b) The UNCITRAL Rules provide a framework for an arbitration which ensures that those matters which must be dealt with in any non-institutional arbitration agreement are dealt with. Nevertheless they leave the parties with considerable flexibility as to how the proceedings are to be conducted.

(c) The UNCITRAL Rules were prepared in consultation with lawyers from many different backgrounds. They should therefore prove acceptable to any *bona fide* party contemplating non-institutional arbitration, regardless of their legal background.

This is not the place for a detailed analysis of the UNCITRAL Arbitration Rules, which cover all the essential matters. Two particular aspects deserve mention:

(a) If the parties fail to agree upon how arbitrators are to be appointed, or how challenges to them are to be dealt with, the Rules provide that one of the parties must request the Secretary-General of the Permanent Court of Arbitration at The Hague to designate an appointing authority (Articles 6(2) and 12(1), respectively). This could lead to some delay in getting the proceedings going. The problem can be avoided if the parties agree at the outset on an appointing authority.

(b) When there are three arbitrators, the award must be made by a majority (Article 31(1)). This differs from the position under the ICC and LCIA Arbitration Rules, which give the chairman of the tribunal the power to make the award alone if there is disagreement between all three arbitrators. The UNCITRAL Arbitration Rules can result in delay whilst the chairman negotiates agreement with the arbitrator whose views most closely approximate to the chairman's.

The UNCITRAL Arbitration Rules may be modified by agreement between the parties, thus providing them with an opportunity to avoid these potential problems. Furthermore, the UNCITRAL Working Group on Arbitration does, from time to time, review the operation of the Rules, and of the Model Law (see below). It is considering proposals for amendment that would cover, *inter alia*, arbitration agreements concluded by an electronic exchange (rather than in writing) and interim measures of protection (perhaps even *ex parte*).

The UNCITRAL Model Law

Apart from drafting a set of rules, UNCITRAL has attempted to provide a solution to the widely shared concerns relating to the actual quality (or lack) of arbitration laws in some states. Two specific needs were identified:

(a) to improve the adequacy of the laws relating to arbitration in a number of states; and

(b) to harmonise state laws on arbitration, thus removing some of the uncertainty that one or other of the parties might feel about the law relating to the arbitration.

The technique adopted by UNCITRAL to deal with this was to prepare a Model Law (published in 1985) which states were encouraged to adopt as their law of arbitration. As an inducement to adopt it, states were not obliged, as they would be with a multilateral convention (subject to specified reservations), to incorporate the Model Law into their own law in its entirety. Rather, states may depart from it to the extent they considered necessary to accommodate important elements of their own law or policy which would otherwise be in conflict with it. This raises an important practical consideration. The fact that a state has adopted the Model Law should not lead to the assumption that the relevant legislation will be a perfect mirror of the Model Law. It may not be, and should therefore be checked. A list of the states which have adopted the Model Law as the basis of their own law of arbitration is set out in Appendix 2.

There is insufficient space here to consider the detailed provisions of the Model Law, but the principal objectives adopted by UNCITRAL in their preparation were:

(a) to limit the role of state courts and to give primacy to the will of the parties in establishing the procedure for the settlement of their disputes;

(b) to secure procedural fairness by means of a limited number of provisions from which the parties could not agree to depart; and

(c) to put in place rules which would permit the completion of an arbitration, even if the parties have not reached agreement on all relevant procedural matters.

CHAPTER 3

THE ARBITRATION AGREEMENT

INTRODUCTION

As indicated in Chapter 1, the aim of this book is to provide an overview of the most significant aspects of international commercial arbitration. Arbitration agreements clearly merit being described as significant. Unfortunately, they are often dealt with at the end of negotiations, when the negotiators are tired. However, arbitration agreements require care and attention: if disputes do arise, the agreement will assume great importance.

Chapter 1 discussed why parties may prefer arbitration to court proceedings. The aim of this chapter is to consider the factors relevant to drafting an agreement to refer future disputes to arbitration. Similar issues arise in the context of an agreement to refer existing disputes to arbitration but if the parties are still on good enough terms to reach such an agreement, it is likely that most of the problems identified below will be easily resolved. A few states around the world still require that an agreement to arbitrate be made only after the dispute has arisen.

This chapter will seek to address the following:

(a) the requirements for a valid and effective arbitration agreement;
(b) important choices which must be made in an arbitration agreement (including the seat of the arbitration and whether the arbitration is to be administered by an arbitral institution); and
(c) issues particularly associated with multi-party arbitration.

Suggested, and standard, clauses dealing with the issues raised in this chapter are included as Appendices 4, 5 and 6.

REQUIREMENTS FOR A VALID AND EFFECTIVE ARBITRATION AGREEMENT

The requirement for writing

In the modern international commercial world, oral contracts may be unusual but are not unknown. However, if parties agree to refer disputes to arbitration, they must ensure that the agreement is in writing. Apart from the obvious advantages of clarity and the avoidance of disputes regarding the terms of the arbitration agreement, there are two main reasons for this.

First, one of the major advantages of arbitration over court proceedings is that it allows the successful party to take advantage of the New York Convention on enforcement of the award. The New York Convention has been widely ratified and makes enforcement much easier than it would otherwise be. However, since Article II of that Convention states that it applies to an "agreement in writing", it will not be possible to rely on the Convention if there is no such written agreement.

Secondly, the UNCITRAL Model Law also requires that an arbitration agreement be in writing. Therefore, an oral arbitration agreement may not be enforceable in Model Law countries or, indeed, the many other countries which have a requirement that arbitration agreements (or contracts generally) be in writing.

There has been much discussion of what constitutes "in writing", particularly in the electronic context in which so many now live. For example, would an exchange of emails be sufficient to satisfy the requirement? The prudent approach is to ensure that the agreement is unambiguously recorded in a recognised form of writing such as a written contract signed by all parties.

Many international companies incorporate into their contracts a reference to a separate document containing standard terms and conditions of contract, or a reference to the terms of another agreement, either of which may contain an arbitration agreement. Such references cannot always be relied upon to create an arbitration agreement "in writing" between the parties to the contract. A party seeking to ensure that an arbitration agreement is effectively made in these circumstances should:

(a) include an express arbitration agreement in the principal contract with the other party; or

(b) include in the principal contract a clear express reference to the arbitration agreement itself which is contained in the other document or contract, and to its incorporation into the principal contract.

Some states have special requirements as to the form of arbitration agreements (for example, that there must be a submission agreement). If the agreement needs to be effective in an unusual jurisdiction, relevant local advice should be obtained.

Effective submission of disputes

If the first requirement of a valid arbitration agreement is that it is in writing, the second is that it is effective to submit the parties' disputes to arbitration. An arbitration will not be properly commenced unless there is an enforceable agreement to refer disputes to arbitration. Factors which may prevent the arbitration agreement being effective include:

(a) lack of capacity of one of the parties to enter into an arbitration agreement (see page 12 above);

(b) the disputes (existing or contemplated) are not arbitrable under the law applicable to the arbitration agreement, the law of the seat (the state in which the arbitration proceedings are to, or are deemed to, take place) or the law of the state in which enforcement is required (see page 13 above); and/or

(c) lack of authority of the representative of a party to enter into the arbitration agreement.

Even if there is no such factor which might prevent the making of an enforceable arbitration agreement, the arbitration agreement, as drafted, may be so muddled, unclear or incomplete that it is not effective to cover all the disputes which the parties intend to submit to arbitration. Such unsatisfactory clauses are widespread and have become known as "pathological" clauses.

The usual causes of difficulty in drafting include:

(a) The parties fail to make a clear, unambiguous and mandatory submission of disputes to arbitration. For example, a clause which provides that "disputes arising out of this agreement may be referred to arbitration" (i.e. not in a mandatory form) might not be effective in preventing one party going to a state court to have the disputes resolved there. The attitude of the local courts to such a clause would be crucial.

(b) The parties fail to include within the scope of the arbitration agreement all of the types of dispute that are likely to arise between them and which they wish to have arbitrated. A submission to arbitration of claims which is restricted to those "arising under this contract" would probably exclude from the jurisdiction of an arbitration any claims for fraud or misrepresentation in the making of the contract.

Examples of clear, widely drawn and mandatory submissions to arbitration may be found in the standard clauses contained in Appendices 4 to 6. These include standard clauses published by the leading arbitral institutions.

IMPORTANT CHOICES IN AN ARBITRATION AGREEMENT

The place (or "seat") of the arbitration

The proposed seat of an intended arbitration is an extremely important choice in the making of any arbitration agreement. Notwithstanding a recent trend toward "delocalisation" of arbitration proceedings (see page 13), the accepted view is that an arbitration must juridically be rooted in a particular jurisdiction (known as the "seat" of the arbitration) and must be conducted in accordance with the arbitration law of that jurisdiction. This does not mean that meetings and hearings conducted by the arbitral tribunal cannot physically take place outside the seat, but simply that the juridical root of the arbitration provides the arbitral legal framework applicable to the arbitration.

As already mentioned (on page 6), countries which have adopted the UNCITRAL Model Law and most other states with modern arbitration laws require two basic principles in relation to arbitration having its seat in that state. First, the parties should be free to agree how their disputes are resolved subject only to certain basic safeguards. Secondly, the courts should interfere with the arbitral process as little as possible, again subject only to certain basic safeguards.

The seat of the arbitration has an impact on three distinct stages of the arbitral process: the recognition of the arbitration agreement, the proceedings, and the recognition or enforcement of the award.

Recognition of the arbitration agreement

The courts of the state which is seat of the arbitration must recognise and give effect to arbitration agreements. The courts of contracting states to the New York Convention are obliged to do so (Article II). However, even those courts will not enforce an agreement for the arbitration of disputes which are not arbitrable under their law and they will set aside any award purportedly made in pursuance of such an agreement.

The courts of many states, particularly those which are parties to the New York Convention, will ensure that a claimant cannot continue to litigate, in the state courts, a dispute governed by a valid and enforceable arbitration agreement and which the respondent insists should be arbitrated. In such a case, effect is usually given to the arbitration agreement by seeking an order "staying" the proceedings, i.e. preventing the claimant from continuing with them, from the court in which the proceedings have been commenced.

The proceedings

The law applicable to the arbitration proceedings will be the arbitration law of the seat. As noted above, arbitrations are conducted most effectively in those seats whose laws and courts favour arbitration as a means of dispute resolution; and therefore respect party autonomy and interfere as little as possible in the proceedings. Some negative examples of interference or restrictions in arbitration proceedings include:

    (a) the local law may impose restrictions on those who may represent the parties (in some countries, only lawyers admitted to the local bar can directly represent the parties in the arbitration, regardless of the law applicable to the dispute, which may increase the time and expense of the arbitration);

    (b) the local law may impose restrictions on who may serve as arbitrator, thus limiting the parties' choice to have the dispute arbitrated in the way that they would wish;

(c) the local law may impose mandatory rules on the manner in which arbitration proceedings may be conducted, for example, by requiring that certain rules (perhaps reflecting local court procedures) be followed.

Each of the issues above may give rise to problems during the course of the proceedings and furthermore, if such local laws are not respected, are likely to cause further problems on recognition or enforcement.

There is also a tactical element to choosing the seat of the arbitration. Certain jurisdictions are known to favour the claimant more than other jurisdictions. Although these differences are more pronounced in court proceedings, some of the same attitudes persist in arbitral proceedings. If one party is much more likely to be the claimant than the other, it is important to consider the following issues.

(a) Does local legal practice usually require the losing party to pay the winning party's costs? If so, will the courts order a claimant to provide security for the legal costs of the respondent? Conversely, can the courts order the respondent to provide security for the claim?

(b) Does local law, regardless of the law applicable to the substance of the disputes themselves, confer any unusual powers on the arbitral tribunal to award damages? In the United States, arbitrators may make awards for punitive damages, unless the parties expressly agree otherwise (although it may well be difficult to enforce any awards for punitive damages – many countries, such as, for example, Japan, have determined that punitive damages are against public policy).

The questions set out above all relate to the legal context in which the proceedings are to be conducted. The administrative context and infrastructure of the proposed location for the proceedings should also be considered. Such a location may (if the arbitration law of seat and/or the parties' arbitration agreement so allows) be a place other than the seat. Does that location have:

(a) a suitable venue for the arbitration, including suitable accommodation for the parties and their witnesses?

(b) reliable communications with the home bases of the parties?

(c) adequate facilities available for support staff?

A further practical issue is that if the location is far from the parties' home bases, then moving representatives, counsel, witnesses and arbitrators to that place will be disproportionately expensive. This disadvantage may be partly offset if suitable counsel and arbitrators are available locally.

Recognition or enforcement of the award

The attitude of various jurisdictions to the upholding and enforcement of awards varies widely. The two key issues are (a) the state courts' attitudes towards appeals and (b) "public policy".

In most states with modern arbitration laws, the right of appeal to the courts from an arbitration award is highly restricted. Indeed, the UNCITRAL Model Law contains no right of appeal and awards can only be set aside on the grounds allowed for in the New York Convention. English law still permits appeals on a point of law but this can be excluded by the parties (and usually is, especially if institutional rules are used). However, even where appeals are excluded, the state courts may still be able to set aside an award on "public policy" grounds. Although this ground is internationally recognised in the UNCITRAL Model Law and the New York Convention, local interpretations vary widely. For example, in *Siemens AG* v. *Dutco* (French Cour de Cassation, 7 January 1992) (discussed further in the section of this chapter relating to multi-party arbitrations), the French Cour de Cassation held that the method of appointment of arbitrators was in breach of French public policy and refused to uphold the award. An even more extreme example was the Indian case of *Oil & Natural Gas Co. Ltd* v. *Saw Pipes Ltd* (Indian Supreme Court, 17 April 2003) which may well widen the definition of public policy to such a degree that it effectively allows appeals on a point of law.

If the arbitration is not to be held in a state in which the respondent has sufficient assets to meet an award, it should at least be held in a state which, together with the state in which the assets are located, is party to an international treaty for the recognition or enforcement of arbitration awards. The best known of these treaties is the New York Convention, but bilateral treaties may also be useful (see pages 20 and 136).

The absence of a treaty allowing enforcement need not always prove fatal to attempts to enforce an award. In such a case the laws of the state in which enforcement will be sought must be considered (see page 123 below). Even if enforcement is available, in the absence of a convention or bilateral treaty it will be much more uncertain. The best approach is to provide for arbitration in one of the contracting states to the New York Convention as this tends to give the widest range of enforcement options (and should also ensure that the state courts uphold and give effect to the arbitration award as discussed above).

It is often difficult to find a state which is satisfactory in every respect and a balance will have to be struck. In striking the balance, it must be borne in mind that the primary objective is an award which is enforceable against the respondent's assets. States whose laws, whether by provision or omission, place an obstacle (such as a refusal to accept the arbitrability of the disputes) in the way of attaining that objective should be avoided.

"Institutional" (administered) or "non-institutional" (*ad hoc*) arbitration

Even though a decision may have been taken to have disputes, whether already existing or arising in the future, submitted to arbitration, work cannot begin on the drafting of the arbitration agreement until the parties have decided whether the arbitration is to be administered by, and pursuant to the rules and procedures, of an arbitration institution (an "institutional" arbitration); or alternatively is to be administered by the arbitral tribunal and the parties (an *ad hoc* or "non-institutional" arbitration).

Institutional arbitration

There are around the world many arbitration institutions, the best known of which are probably, as mentioned in Chapter 1, the ICC, the LCIA and the ICDR (the international arm of the AAA). As already noted, ICSID administers the arbitration of investment disputes involving states or state bodies. There are also regional or national institutions, such as the Chamber of Commerce and Industry of the Russian Federation, the Stockholm Chamber of Commerce (often popular with ex-CIS states), the Hong Kong International Arbitration Centre (the "HKIAC"), the China International Economic and Trade Arbitration Commission ("CIETAC"), the Singapore Arbitration Centre and the Australian Centre for International Commercial Arbitration. Finally, there are specialist institutions with arbitration expertise, such as for example the World Intellectual Property Organisation ("WIPO") and many trade associations. Notable examples are the various commodity trade bodies such as, for example, the Grain and Feed Trade Association ("GAFTA") and shipping institutions such as, for example, the London Maritime Arbitrators Association.

The principal reasons for considering why institutional arbitration should be used at all include the following:

(a) An institution is particularly helpful at the commencement of an arbitration because it can ensure that a tribunal is appointed without recourse to the state courts (such recourse, in any event, not being available in all states). This is a major advantage – the alternative is often a long procedural wrangle when the claimant would much rather be progressing with the actual claim. Even if the parties decide on non-institutional, that is *ad hoc*, arbitration, it is often useful to provide for one of the leading arbitral bodies to act as appointing authority to constitute the tribunal (see below).

(b) In addition to making it easier to appoint a tribunal, a good institution will ensure that the tribunal is independent, impartial and suitable for the dispute referred. The involvement of an institution should ensure that even party-appointed arbitrators are genuinely independent (which may not always be the case in a non-institutional process).

(c) The institution will handle the money, arrange for payment of expenses and fix the fees of the arbitrators. This institutional role in relation to the fees of arbitrators is useful in controlling costs and also avoids the awkward issue of the parties to the dispute having to discuss fees directly with the tribunal who will be deciding the dispute.

(d) A good institution will also provide a resource for the arbitrators. It may provide administrative support and also assistance with difficult issues arising in the proceedings.

(e) The arbitration rules of the leading institutions should cover all the necessary elements to allow the efficient conduct of an arbitration from the commencement of proceedings through to the making of an enforceable award. The rules contain provisions which will ensure that a tribunal is appointed to deal with the arbitration, that a party cannot frustrate the arbitration by refusing to co-operate and that an arbitrator cannot do so either. Since 1976, and the publication of the UNCITRAL Arbitration Rules for incorporation in non-institutional arbitration agreements, this particular reason has assumed a lesser importance, because the arbitration agreement can incorporate the UNCITRAL Arbitration Rules. One advantage of the institutional rules over the UNCITRAL Arbitration Rules is that they can be updated whenever an issue arises which may affect the conduct of future arbitrations. For example, the institutions were quick to update their rules following the decision in the *Dutco* case (see page 41 below), which cast doubt on methods of appointing arbitrators in a multi-party case.

(f) By using a well-respected institution, the successful party benefits from a perception that the procedure was legitimate and fair. From a strict legal standpoint, it should not matter whether or not the arbitration was administered by an institution. However, there is certainly a view that courts may well start from the position that an ICC or LCIA award should be upheld whereas they may be more sceptical of a non-institutional arbitration.

These benefits come at a price – institutional arbitration may be more expensive because, in addition to the fees of the arbitrators and the costs of the venue, the institution itself must be paid for the administrative service it provides. There is the additional possible disadvantage that the administrative procedures can be time consuming and are therefore not suited to arbitrations where speed is of the essence. This is particularly the case when (as is the case with the ICC) the institution takes a role in reviewing the tribunal's award. However, many institutions (including the ICC) have responded to this criticism by developing expedited procedures.

Notwithstanding the cost of administrative fees (and possibly time), the better view is that the advantages of institutional arbitration outlined above make this the preferred choice in agreements for the submission of future disputes. An efficiently administered arbitration which is kept to a reasonable timetable will quite possibly recoup, by way of saved legal expenses, the administrative fees.

Turning to the institutions themselves, the choice of institution will have to be made in the light of the particular circumstances of the case. A contract involving a state or state body may be steered toward ICSID, because of the strong provisions of the Washington Convention relating to the enforcement of awards. Disputes between parties domiciled in a particular region may by inclination go to that region's arbitration centre. Caution is advised if considering using a small regional or national arbitration centre – it may not have the necessary experience or expertise in dealing with international arbitration and, in the worst case, might even cease to exist by the time of the dispute.

A factor in the choice of institution will be the arbitration rules it applies. Those of the leading institutions adopt a broadly similar approach, but there are differences between them and not just on minor points of detail. It is also important to consider the institution's general approach to procedure (whether or not provided for in the written rules). For example, those of the LCIA are more detailed and prescriptive than those of the ICC. Institutions such as the LCIA and the AAA/ICDR are also prepared to administer arbitrations conducted under the UNCITRAL Arbitration Rules rather than their own. Appendix 3 contains a comparative analysis of some of the most significant arbitration rules of the ICC, the LCIA, the AAA/ICDR and UNCITRAL.

The rules need to be checked for any unusual features. It is also important to read and understand the "default" provisions – i.e. what the position will be if the parties do not specifically provide in their agreement for a particular issue. For example, Article 35 of the Arbitration Rules of CIETAC provides that, unless otherwise agreed by the parties, hearings shall be in Beijing, or in other places with the approval of the Secretary General of the Arbitration Commission. Similarly, Article 16 of the LCIA Arbitration Rules provides that, in default of agreement of the parties, the seat of the arbitration will be London unless otherwise ordered by the LCIA Court.

The arbitration rules of the internationally recognised institutions, such as, for example, the ICC and the LCIA, have been drafted so as to provide a self-contained code, in each case, for the effective and efficient conduct of an international commercial arbitration. It is therefore usually sufficient to use the standard arbitration clause of the chosen institution – in the sense that the clause will be sufficient to submit disputes to an arbitration pursuant to the rules of the institution which should result in an award. Indeed, trying to introduce detailed procedural prescriptions into institutional arbitration agreements is generally not recommended because it may not be possible to comply with them and they may even conflict with the institution's rules. The standard arbitration clauses published by the ICC, the AAA/ICDR and the LCIA are to be found in Appendix 4, along with suggestions to deal with the important subjects of the number of arbitrators and the place and language of the arbitration.

When one uses an unfamiliar institution, its arbitration rules should always be checked to ensure that there are no serious gaps in them. Useful standards by which to judge them are the arbitration rules of the ICC, the LCIA, the AAA/ICDR or the UNCITRAL Arbitration Rules.

Non-institutional arbitration

The advantages and disadvantages of non-institutional arbitration (that is, an *ad hoc* arbitration which is administered by the arbitral tribunal and the parties, not by an arbitral institution) are the converse of those for institutional arbitration.

One particular circumstance in which non-institutional arbitration has an advantage is when it is used in connection with a dispute which has already come into existence. Knowing what the dispute is, and being aware of the circumstances surrounding it (such as the amount of relevant documentation and the number of potential witnesses), the parties can design specific rules to suit the requirements of the particular dispute. They can, for example, spell out the scope of disclosure obligations and establish appropriate time limits for the arbitration. In doing so, they may use (indeed, should at the very least consider) the UNCITRAL Arbitration Rules, modifying them to suit their purpose. The advantage of doing this is that provision for important issues in the arbitration procedure will not be overlooked. They may also consider the broadly similar, but more recent (1992), CPR Institute for Dispute Resolution Rules for Non-Administered Arbitration of International Disputes. If the parties are to use an entirely tailor-made procedure rather than rely on one of these self-contained codes, the submission agreement will be extensive and will need to be drafted carefully to ensure that it provides everything necessary for the smooth running of the arbitration and the enforcement of the award.

There is an additional matter which must be taken into account: the identity of the institution or person designated to appoint members of the arbitral tribunal (or fill vacancies) in the absence of agreement between the parties, or of a nomination by one of them where it has the right to nominate an arbitrator. (In the case of institutional arbitration, the institution itself will perform this role.) Some arbitration institutions, such as the ICC and the LCIA, are prepared to act as the appointing authority, even when an arbitration has not been subjected to their rules. They charge a fee for this service. Where a dispute will be connected with a particular industry, it is common for the president of the relevant industry association to be designated as the appointing authority (for example, "the President of the Institution of Civil Engineers" in the case of a construction dispute). However, make sure that any body proposed as an appointing authority is competent to perform this task.

If non-institutional arbitration has been chosen because of a desire to have an arbitration procedure which reflects the circumstances of the particular disputes which are likely to arise, a tailor-made agreement should be prepared. The drafting of any such agreement will necessarily turn on the circumstances of the anticipated disputes and no more than general guidance can be proffered. A draft non-institutional arbitration clause is included at Appendix 6. Because individual solutions are required, that draft should not be followed unthinkingly. So that the draft can provide real assistance, it has been broken up, by the use of headings, into the principal elements which have to be considered. Each element has been cross-referenced to that part of the main text which deals with it, so that the relevant considerations can be taken into account.

A note of caution

One of the most important things to remember about non-institutional arbitration is that there is no arbitration institution to assist the parties if difficulties arise and it may well be that the state courts may not offer useful assistance either. It is therefore important to ensure that adequate provision is made for contingencies which could otherwise put a halt to the arbitration (such as, for example, the death of the arbitrator), and that the agreement remains sufficiently flexible to take account of changing circumstances. For example, parties are perfectly entitled to expect arbitrators to make their awards expeditiously. However, requiring them to do so within a fixed period of time, whilst making no provision for the extension of that period, could have the result that the arbitrators are found to have ceased to have jurisdiction if they exceed the period.

The governing law of the contract and arbitration agreement

The governing law of the contract and that of the arbitration agreement should always be specified in order to avoid arguments later as to what they are. It is, however, usual for parties to specify the applicable law in their principal agreement and not in the arbitration agreement. Mention has already been made of some of the ways in which parties can modify or supplement the applicable law (see pages 15 and 16 above).

The law applicable to the substance of the dispute may have little bearing on the arbitration procedure itself (as opposed to its outcome). In most cases, the law which is applicable to the principal agreement will also be applicable to the arbitration agreement (although under the doctrine of the separability of the arbitration agreement, this is not necessarily the case – see page 12 above). Unless there are special circumstances, the usual position is sensible and less likely to cause disputes than having different laws governing the principal agreement and the arbitration agreement.

One circumstance in which parties sometimes provide for different laws to govern the principal agreement and the arbitration agreement is when the law governing the principal agreement prohibits the arbitration of the kind of disputes which may arise. In those circumstances, parties may provide that the arbitration agreement is to be governed by some other system of law which permits arbitration of those disputes.

However, in the situation envisaged above, the courts of the state whose law has been chosen to apply to the principal agreement may claim jurisdiction (on the ground that that law is also applicable to the arbitration agreement) to deal with applications to set aside any award made. In most cases, it would be better to change the governing law of the principal agreement to one which regarded all disputes likely to arise as arbitrable.

The number of arbitrators

It is often suggested that large and important disputes should be submitted for arbitration by three arbitrators (usually with each of the two parties nominating an arbitrator and the third being agreed by the parties or their nominated arbitrators, or appointed by the institution administering the arbitration), whilst less significant disputes should be dealt with by a sole arbitrator.

However, parties should not follow this approach unthinkingly, particularly where speed is important. Good arbitrators tend to be busy arbitrators. Trying to fix dates for hearings when all three arbitrators are available at the same time can be a difficult task and can extend the length of the arbitration considerably. Furthermore, arbitrators try to reach a consensus if possible which can delay the production of interim and final awards. Cost is also significant. However, constituting a tribunal with three arbitrators may greatly enhance the quality of the procedure and the award. It may also create an incentive against delay in performance that might otherwise be suffered with a sole arbitrator.

It is not recommended to name in advance individuals to act as arbitrators in an agreement to deal with future disputes. Arbitrators are not immortal and the death of the arbitrator may frustrate the operation of the arbitration clause. One approach which is sometimes used in circumstances where the parties want to control the identity of the arbitrator is to specify a list of individuals regarded as suitable.

The language of the arbitration

The purpose of such a provision is self-evident. It is usually appropriate to have the language of the arbitration follow that of the contract, and that in which the business relationship has been conducted. This will reduce the amount of translation work that has to be done, which is usually very costly.

Multi-tiered dispute resolution clauses

There is a growing trend in international contracts for provision to be made for a series of steps to be taken before either party resorts to arbitration. For example, the contract may require the parties to engage in negotiations and then mediation before arbitration proceedings can be commenced. Multi-tiered dispute resolution clauses, and some of the issues associated with them, are discussed in more detail on pages 56–59.

Miscellaneous matters

There are a number of other matters which it may be appropriate to deal with in the arbitration agreement. These may depend on the law of the arbitration proceedings, on the law of the place of enforcement of the award, and any institutional rules used. They include the following.

(a) *State immunity*: If the one of the parties to the arbitration agreement is a state, that party should be expected to waive both its immunity to the jurisdiction of the courts of the seat of the arbitration (insofar as they have jurisdiction to deal with matters arising out of the arbitration, such as the replacement of an arbitrator guilty of misconduct) and its immunity from execution in respect of any award made against it.

(b) *Procedural rules*: If the arbitration is to be non-institutional and without reference to an established body of rules, basic procedural requirements should be laid out, taking care not to be over-prescriptive. In contrast, if institutional rules are used, they address the necessary procedural framework and trying to introduce separate procedural requirements in the arbitration agreement is likely to be counter-productive.

(c) *Security for claim*: In the United States an arbitral tribunal may have power to order a respondent insurer to provide security for the claim. Any party carrying a contingent obligation to indemnify another should consider incorporating into an agreement for arbitration in the US a specific exclusion of that power to order security.

(d) *Security for costs*: The tribunal may be given the power to order the claimant to give security for the respondent's legal costs in the event that the claimant is unsuccessful in the arbitration (see, for example, Article 25(2) of the LCIA Arbitration Rules).

(e) *Amiable composition*: As mentioned on page 16 above, this is the power which may be conferred by agreement on an arbitral tribunal to arrive at a decision which it thinks is fair, even if it is not strictly in accordance with the applicable law. Generally, this is not recommended because of the uncertainty which it can introduce.

(f) *Confidentiality*: Arbitration is generally regarded as a private process (e.g. the public is excluded from the hearings). Until fairly recently, it was also widely assumed that confidentiality was an essential characteristic of international commercial arbitration (e.g. documents produced in the course of the arbitration, or statements made at the hearings, could not be made public by either party). This assumption is now open to doubt following the decisions of the High Court of Australia in *Esso/BHP* v. *Plowman* (1995) and the Supreme Court of Sweden in *AI Trade Finance Inc.* v. *Bulgarian Foreign Trade Bank (Bulbank) Ltd* (2000). If parties want to be sure that their arbitration will be confidential, they should now expressly make it so in their arbitration agreement (see, for example, Article 30 of the LCIA Arbitration Rules). The position in England was clarified in *Ali Shipping Corp.* v. *Shipyard Trogir* (1998), when the English Court of Appeal confirmed that an obligation of confidentiality is to be implied into arbitration agreements governed by English law. However, doubt was cast on that approach by the Privy Council in *Associated Electric and Gas Insurance Services* v. *European Reinsurance Co. of Zurich* (29 January 2003). The Privy Council seemed to suggest that the correct course would be to consider whether there was an obligation of confidentiality relating to the specific documents in respect of which confidentiality was asserted, rather than seeking to argue that the documents fell within an exception to an obligation of confidentiality presumed to exist as an implied term of the arbitration agreement.

MULTI-PARTY ARBITRATION

Introduction

Arbitration, as we have seen, arises as a matter of contract between the parties to an arbitration agreement and therefore the proceedings and outcome usually bind only those parties to the arbitration. That principle can give rise to complications in arbitrations arising out of multi-party contracts or chains of contracts (i.e. where more than two entities are involved). The main circumstances in which more than two entities may be involved include the following:

(a) Where there is a chain of separate contracts, such as in commodity dealing, or in construction projects. In a chain of separate contracts, the subject-matter of a dispute between A and B will often be the same as, or similar to, the subject-matter of a dispute between B and C. In such a case, there are obvious advantages if the award between B and C is consistent with the award between A and B. In addition, it will obviously be more efficient, and will save costs, if the disputes can be heard by the same arbitral tribunal, and at the same time. For tactical reasons, however (such as a desire for delay, or dislike of an arbitrator), C may not be prepared to agree to this. Furthermore, A might be concerned about the effect that a complicated factual dispute between B and C might have on the progress (and cost) of the resolution of its dispute with B.

(b) Where a number of organisations or individuals join together in a single contract, such as in a consortium or partnership arrangement, within a consortium or partnership arrangement one entity might wish to bring a claim against two or more of the others, and those claims may not be identical. Again, it will be more efficient to have the disputes heard by the same arbitral tribunal, and at the same time.

Problems of multi-party arbitration

The broad nature of the problems of multi-party arbitration was well illustrated in the following comments made by an English judge in *Oxford Shipping Co. Ltd* v. *Nippon Yusen Kaisha* (1984):

"Arbitrators enjoy no power to order concurrent hearings, or anything of that nature, without the consent of the parties. The concept of private arbitrations derives simply from the fact that the parties have agreed to submit to arbitration particular disputes arising between them and only between them. It is implicit in this that strangers shall be excluded from the hearing and conduct of the arbitration and that neither the tribunal nor any of the parties can insist that the dispute shall be heard or determined concurrently with or even in consonance with another dispute, however convenient that course may be to the party seeking it and however closely associated the disputes in question may be."

The above comments indicate the strong basis for a third party's objection to being brought into a multi-party arbitration against its wishes. In the discussion of differences between arbitration and court proceedings set out in Chapter 1, we cited both the control of the parties over the arbitration process, and its private (and perhaps confidential) nature. These are important principles of arbitration. They are also often a reason that parties prefer arbitration to court proceedings. For example, large commercial organisations do not necessarily want third parties gaining an insight into their business dealings.

In certain circumstances, multi-party arbitrations may well go against the general principles of the control of the parties and privacy in arbitrations. Another key principle of arbitration (and dispute resolution generally) is that the parties must be treated equally by the tribunal. In certain circumstances, this principle of party equality may also be threatened by a multi-party arbitration procedure. This means that there is a distinct tension between the desire to improve efficiency by resolving all disputes in one forum and a concern to uphold the key principles of arbitration outlined above. The rules of leading arbitral institutions and decisions of state courts discussed below often reflect this tension.

The reason why problems frequently arise is that arbitration agreements very rarely provide for such problems and even more rarely contain adequate provisions to deal with them. This is not surprising: the detailed wording of the arbitration provision often receives scant attention when a contract is being negotiated and the provisions that may be needed to deal adequately with multi-party arbitration are complicated. For those reasons, they are often ignored. However, the problems of multi-party arbitration can be anticipated and provision can be made in the arbitration agreement to deal with them. Such provisions are discussed below.

Best solution

As hinted at in (a) on page 38 above, the best solution, where there is a chain of contracts, is to require the parties to all such contracts to enter into an arbitration agreement (which can be by way of an identical clause included in each of the contracts) by which they agree to be joined as parties in an arbitration between other parties to the chain of contracts, and in connection with disputes arising out of such contracts, and to be bound by the award made in that arbitration. In the case of a consortium agreement, the parties are already subject to a single contract and it is only necessary to ensure that the arbitration agreement is sufficiently well-drafted to deal with the issues which may arise.

If the solution of a single arbitration agreement covering all disputes is adopted, there is sometimes a tendency for all parties to be drawn in, even though some may not be affected by the dispute at all and others only to a limited extent. If, for example, A has a dispute with B and a different dispute with C, should A commence one arbitration against both B and C, or should it commence separate arbitrations against each of them? Many arbitration clauses simply refer to "any dispute" and require it to be referred to arbitration. It would be more helpful to the parties, at least in cases where two or more individual members may become involved, for the clause to be more specific and deal expressly with the situation where there may be a number of disputes, not all of them between the same parties.

The arbitration clause should aim to give clear guidance as to how such associated arbitrations are to proceed and the extent to which such arbitrations are to be integrated or consolidated by reason of the relationship between the parties under the applicable agreement(s).

If it is apparent at the start of the arbitration between A and B that the dispute is likely to involve other contracting parties then, provided that the rules of the arbitration give the tribunal the necessary power, the tribunal may try to avert the procedural problems that are likely to arise by:

(a) requiring A to narrow its claim to matters only relevant to B; or
(b) inviting A to claim against all of the other relevant consortium members as multiple respondents.

An arbitration agreement which provides for a single arbitration in a consortium or chain situation must provide, in the absence of agreement between all of the parties, for the nomination of the arbitrator(s) to decide the dispute. The way in which this is done is one of the more difficult aspects of a multi-party arbitration agreement.

Appointment of arbitrators

The major issue concerning the appointment of arbitrators in these circumstances is that not all the parties will necessarily be in a position effectively to express a view on the nomination. Each arbitration clause must make provision for this. Incautious drafting of the arbitration agreement can lead to problems in appointing the tribunal.

Arbitration agreements in international commerce often stipulate expressly, or by implication, that each party is to have a degree of choice or say in the selection of the arbitrator or arbitrators. It is the same with the rules of many international arbitration institutions. In chain contracts, a party who is to be added to an arbitration already proceeding between parties to another contract in the chain can have no say in the choice of arbitrator and must consent (or be required by the terms of the arbitration clause included in his contract to consent) to the existing arbitrator(s) and to the procedure already adopted. This difficulty is exacerbated if the arbitration agreement calls for a tribunal of three arbitrators, each party appointing one, and those two arbitrators then appointing the third.

Another way in which the difficulty manifests itself is when the claimant, in its request for arbitration submitted to an institution (as under the rules of the ICC and the LCIA) nominates an arbitrator. Where there are two or more respondents and they are unable to agree upon the second arbitrator (in the case of a tribunal consisting of three arbitrators), the institution may nominate an arbitrator on their behalf. This second scenario was exactly the position in the noted French case of *Siemens AG* v. *Dutco*. In that case, the two respondents had failed to agree on an arbitrator and accordingly the ICC Court had nominated one on their behalf. The respondents later challenged the award obtained before the French courts. The Cour de Cassation (the highest appeal court in France) ruled that the method of appointment of the tribunal breached the principle that the parties should be treated equally in the arbitration because the respondents did not have the same opportunity to influence the composition of the tribunal as the claimant. The court held that breaching the principle of the equality of the parties was against French public policy and the award was therefore invalid. The effect of the decision is wide-ranging in that a number of the usual methods of appointing arbitrators may therefore be invalid in a multi-party situation.

Furthermore, other leading jurisdictions may well take a similar view that such methods of appointment are against public policy. For example, although the position in Germany is unclear, the general view is that in a multi-party situation, it is prudent to use a neutral appointing authority in default of agreement.

In the light of the *Dutco* case, both the ICC and the LCIA introduced revised rules to attempt to avoid the difficulty. In the case of the ICC, Article 10 of its Rules now provides that, in the case of multiple respondents and/or multiple claimants, if such parties cannot agree on a joint nomination, the ICC Court will appoint the entire tribunal. Article 8 of the LCIA Arbitration Rules now provides that in a multi-party arbitration, if the parties to the dispute cannot agree that there are two separate sides to the arbitration as claimant and respondent, then the LCIA Court will appoint the entire tribunal. Arguably, neither of these rules covers the full range of possible problems with the nominations of arbitrators in a multi-party situation but the institutions can be expected to operate the rules in a pragmatic manner by appointing the entire tribunal whenever a situation analogous to the *Dutco* case may occur.

Provided that the problems of appointing the tribunal can be resolved, the best solution remains to have all parties enter into one arbitration agreement to have all disputes resolved in the same forum. However, for the reasons already mentioned such an agreement may not be attractive to all the parties to all the contracts and they may refuse to enter into it. In that event, one must consider the alternatives.

Likewise, if drafting a clause for non-institutional arbitration where a multi-party situation is likely to occur, it is better to avoid the problem by providing that, in default of an agreed procedure for nominations by the parties, a neutral appointing authority (for example, one of the leading arbitration institutions) appoints the entire tribunal.

Subsequent joining of third parties

Problems in enforcing the rules may arise if, as well as referring to the LCIA or ICC rules, the arbitration clause stipulates a particular method of appointing arbitrators which is inconsistent with the method of appointment being used by the LCIA or the ICC.

The problems of multi-party arbitrations do not generally apply in state court proceedings. The procedural rules of many state courts allow the courts to add parties to proceedings and provide for one judge to determine all disputes at one time. Although this resolves the problems of multi-party situations before state courts, arbitration by contrast is entirely a matter of contract. The procedures available in courts to compel the involvement of additional parties are not available to arbitral tribunals unless each arbitration agreement so provides.

A partial exception to this principle of party autonomy has been introduced in the Rules of the LCIA: Article 22.1(h) provides that the tribunal can add third parties to the arbitration if one of the existing parties wants it to do so and the proposed third party agrees (apparently regardless of whether or not the other party to the arbitration agreement objects). The arbitrator(s) can then, according to these rules, make a single award in respect of all the parties to the proceedings – presumably including an award in favour of the third party against the original claimant, who might not have wished the third party to be introduced into the arbitration.

The principle lying behind the new rules of the LCIA appears, at first sight, to go against the basic premise of arbitration, which is that it is a consensual procedure, to be conducted according to the wishes of the parties. In this case, A may find that an award is made against it in favour of C with whom A has no contractual relationship and with whom A has never consented to have its dispute resolved by arbitration (save by A's agreement originally to arbitration pursuant to such rules including such a provision for joinder). Furthermore, if one of the parties seeks to join C to the arbitration after the tribunal was appointed by means of party nominations, then they potentially leave themselves open to a challenge on *Dutco* grounds unless the entire tribunal was replaced by a tribunal appointed by a neutral authority. Some of the new rules (such as those of the LCIA) seek to pre-empt such challenges by providing that by agreeing to arbitrate under the rules the parties agree not to apply to a relevant court for any relief regarding the jurisdiction of the arbitrator(s). It remains to be seen whether such provisions will be effective.

Separate arbitrations

If related disputes are arbitrated separately, the most obvious risk is that different arbitral tribunals will arrive at different findings of fact and different interpretations of the contractual terms, even where the wording is identical. One way of avoiding this is to require the tribunal in the second arbitration to follow and adopt the decisions of the tribunal in the first arbitration, at least where the facts and the contractual terms are the same. A requirement on these lines is rare. Most arbitrators would be reluctant to accept such a limitation on arriving at their own conclusions, feeling that it would severely restrict their ability to do justice between the parties before them and apply the terms of the contract. A further difficulty is that at least one of the parties to the second arbitration will wish to prevent the second tribunal from having to follow any adverse findings made by the first tribunal and will seek to introduce fresh evidence and argue different points on the contract. It will be very difficult for the second tribunal to decide that those facts or arguments are necessarily spurious such that it should ignore them and follow the first tribunal.

A second and more limited approach is to stipulate in the second arbitration agreement that evidence given in the first arbitration shall not only be admissible (i.e. may be used) in the second, but shall also be conclusive evidence in the second arbitration as to the matters it deals with. A provision on these lines avoids some of the points of principle that would give arbitrators difficulties in accepting the solution suggested in the previous paragraph. However, such a stipulation may be difficult to apply in practice, unless the arbitration agreement specifies precisely which evidence, given in the first arbitration, is to be admissible and conclusive in the second – something which it is difficult to provide for at the time that the arbitration agreement is negotiated. Some of the practical questions that would have to be dealt with would include the following.

(a) Are all the documents admitted as evidence in the first arbitration to be admitted in the second?
(b) Is the evidence of all witnesses in the first arbitration to be admitted in the second, or only the evidence relating to the issues in the second? If the latter, how is it to be decided which evidence relates to the issues in the second arbitration?
(c) How is the evidence given in the first arbitration to be recorded? A transcript is likely to be more reliable for use in the second arbitration than a note made by the first tribunal, or by the parties to the first arbitration.

(d) If a witness who gave evidence in the first arbitration has to give further evidence in the second (for example, to deal with an issue not raised in the first), can the evidence previously given be qualified or changed? The tribunal will be most reluctant to prevent a witness changing evidence, but may be constrained from permitting changes by the terms of the arbitration agreement, which governs the arbitral tribunal's jurisdiction in the absence of a further agreement by the parties.

The complicated drafting and requirement to provide for future disputes accurately that would be needed to deal adequately with these points is one of the main reasons why arbitration agreements rarely adopt this approach.

A third way of seeking to avoid inconsistent decisions is to appoint the same arbitral tribunal in both arbitrations. This approach was adopted in the English case of *Abu Dhabi Gas Liquefaction* v. *Eastern Bechtel Corp.* (1982) which concerned linked disputes arising under the main construction contract and a major sub-contract. The Court of Appeal clearly wished that there was a power to consolidate the two arbitrations but settled for appointing the same arbitrator in both cases. Even this approach has limitations, because if the two arbitrations are heard at different times, with different advocates and possibly different or additional witnesses, the arbitral tribunal may feel, when deciding the second arbitration, that it should arrive at a different conclusion from the one it arrived at in the first arbitration. There is also the danger that the tribunal will, in the second arbitration, remember, and apply, evidence given in the first, but which neither party has adduced in the second. The arbitral award would then be open to challenge.

Finally, a solution adopted in commodity arbitrations under rules such as GAFTA is that if the contracts are on the same material terms except for price then the arbitration can be held directly between the parties at the end of the chain. This approach is only likely to be successful if the contracts really are back-to-back and there are no separate issues affecting intermediate parties in the chain.

State court involvement

One of the simplest approaches to resolving the problems of multi-party arbitration is to provide that, if more than two parties are to be involved, the arbitration agreement falls away and the parties have to revert to state court proceedings. Although simple, this is unlikely to be agreed in most cases. The parties may have chosen arbitration in the first case because it avoided having to resort to the courts of a state, or because they wanted any disputes to be decided by someone with particular technical skills. Even if the parties had no particular reason for choosing arbitration, they might each feel that a provision abrogating the arbitration clause if a third party was involved, would be open to abuse, in that it would encourage the party wishing to avoid arbitration to introduce a spurious third party.

Although arbitration is intended to be separate from, and independent of, state courts, the laws of many states give their courts residual rights of supervision over arbitrations proceeding in their territories. Normally these laws relate to such matters as the power to dismiss an arbitrator who behaves improperly, or to lending the assistance of the court to enforce rulings made by the arbitral tribunal. However, a small number of states have passed laws enabling their courts to order the compulsory joinder of arbitrations where three or more parties are involved. Hong Kong was one of the first to introduce a law on these lines, in 1982. The power was limited to domestic arbitrations. In 1986, the Netherlands introduced legislation permitting consolidation of arbitrations (including international arbitrations) by the court, unless the parties have agreed otherwise.

Where these laws apply, they can be very helpful in achieving the goals of consistency in awards and efficiency in the arbitration process. However, they remain tainted by the stigma of a state court system and involve intervention by it. Furthermore, even such laws have difficulty in dealing with some of the problems which may arise, such as where the parties to the various contracts may not all have agreed to arbitration in the same state or the same method of appointing the tribunal. They have therefore found little favour with the majority of states (the point was considered but rejected in the drafting of the English Arbitration Act 1996). Section 35 of the English Act allows the tribunal to consolidate proceedings only if the parties have agreed to give the tribunal that power.

Confidentiality issues

The confidentiality obligations often considered implicit in arbitration agreements may also lead to practical difficulties where two parties seek to resolve a dispute by arbitration in what is commercially a multi-party situation. This may cause difficulties in subsequent arbitrations if a party wants to use documents which were disclosed in the previous arbitration.

Other third party involvement in arbitration

There are a number of other circumstances in which third parties, not originally subject to the arbitration agreement, may become involved.

(a) In England, unless expressly excluded, the Contracts (Rights of Third Parties) Act 1999 enables third parties to enforce the terms of a contract entered into for their benefit. In the case of *Nisshin Shipping Co.* v. *Cleaves & Co.* (2003), the court allowed a third party (in this case, shipbrokers promised commission) to enforce an arbitration clause in a contract. The court held that the shipbrokers were entitled to and indeed obliged to apply the arbitration clause in the contract, notwithstanding that the arbitration clause seemed only to contemplate an arbitration between the parties to the contract. Many other jurisdictions may also allow third parties to enforce contract terms and this may well include the arbitration clause. The same will not be true in all jurisdictions.

(b) A third party may subsequently become, by novation or assignment, a party to an agreement containing an arbitration clause. Under English law, no conceptual issue arises on novation because the new third party is treated as stepping into the position of the former party to the contract and thus is bound by the arbitration agreement. An interesting point arises if a third party is assigned the benefit of an agreement – can they be obliged to proceed with arbitration if this is what the original contract provides? At least under English law, an assignee is obliged to arbitrate in accordance with the original contract (as the Court of Appeal decided in the *The Jaybola* (1997)).

(c) It is also possible for third parties to become parties to arbitration agreements by operation of law (e.g. under an insolvency process). As would be expected, any disputes arising are obliged to be referred to arbitration as they would have been between the original parties.

In conclusion, drafting an effective agreement for multi-party arbitration is fraught with difficulty and is usually best left to those who have experience of drafting such agreements. Indeed, even the ICC working party established to report on multi-party disputes was unable to recommend a form of agreement. However, that working party did publish a report (submitted for adoption by the Executive Board in June 1994) which had attached to it a number of suggested agreements which parties can consider.

CONCLUSION

This chapter has shown the various difficulties involved in drafting an arbitration agreement. However, that said, it is a relatively simple task to create an effective arbitration clause in a two-party dispute either by using an institutional standard clause, by consulting Appendices 4 to 6 of this book or by using a drafting engine such as the one at *www.lovells.com/arbitration*. It is therefore surprising that so many contracts seem to contain defective arbitration clauses. These can usually be made to work but often only after a lengthy and tedious procedural dispute which begins when one party attempts to commence arbitration. If the dispute is of a multi-party nature or there are other unusual circumstances, it is wise to seek professional advice on the drafting of the arbitration agreement.

CHAPTER 4

ADR IN INTERNATIONAL ARBITRATION

INTRODUCTION

Reference was made in Chapter 1 to the availability of alternative (or, amicable) dispute resolution ("ADR") processes, in addition to state court and arbitration proceedings. Whilst this book is essentially concerned with international commercial arbitration, it is nevertheless appropriate to take a brief look at ADR. ADR is now encountered so often, either before the commencement of an arbitration or during the course of one, that anyone having to deal with arbitration should be aware of what it involves. So prevalent is consideration of the use of ADR that provision for its use has been made by the leading arbitral institutions, such as the ICC and LCIA, and by UNCITRAL.

The use of ADR is already well established in the United States and many US states have adopted legislation on mediation, the most common form of ADR. A national Uniform Mediation Act has also now been enacted and is being considered by a number of state legislatures.

ADR is also gaining recognition in Europe, as illustrated by the publication of the European Commission's Green Paper on ADR (primarily mediation) (COM (2002) 196), which launched a consultation process on the harmonisation of legal systems on ADR. As a result of the consultation, the European Commission launched two initiatives: first, to start work on developing a European plan for best practice in mediation; and secondly, to present a proposal for a directive to promote mediation.

At one stage ADR procedures were regarded as including all the different methods for the resolution of disputes other than court proceedings. However, in the international context, arbitration is typically excluded from the definition of ADR procedures. This is in part because the recent popularity of ADR procedures is the result of concern about the length and cost of both court proceedings and arbitration, particularly where there are many factual issues which have to be resolved (as, for example, in construction disputes).

After a brief introduction, highlighting the main differences between ADR and arbitration or court proceedings, this chapter will focus on:

    (a) organisations which offer ADR facilities;

    (b) an explanation of the main forms of ADR;

(c) considerations when selecting a third party neutral; and

(d) contractual clauses providing for ADR as a means of resolving disputes and the enforceability of such clauses.

SOME DIFFERENCES BETWEEN ARBITRATION AND ADR

There are a number of significant differences between court proceedings and arbitration, on the one hand, and some forms of ADR, in particular mediation (the most common form of ADR process), on the other. First, many forms of ADR are not adjudicative processes resulting in a binding determination of the parties' rights and obligations. Secondly, ADR processes such as mediation typically focus on the parties' interests as much as, or more than, on their rights. Thirdly, mediation and other non-adjudicative forms of ADR require the active co-operation of the parties assisted by a third party, such as a mediator, in an attempt to achieve an agreed settlement of their dispute. Agreement is not the inevitable result of a non-adjudicative ADR procedure and the process will break down as soon as one party withdraws its co-operation since no party to such a procedure can be compelled to conclude a settlement agreement.

Thus, unlike state court proceedings or arbitration, ADR because of its consensual nature does not necessarily lead to a resolution of the dispute. If it fails to result in an agreed settlement, the parties will have to fall back on arbitration or state court proceedings to resolve their dispute. This is of particular significance in the international context. Unless the parties have agreed upon a forum (whether the courts of a particular state or arbitration), one of the parties may find that it is compelled to litigate the dispute in a forum which it finds undesirable.

Some ADR procedures, including mediation, often take place concurrently with, or as a prelude to, an arbitration or court proceedings. When they do so, the arbitration or court proceedings may (but may not have to be) put on hold until the ADR procedure has been brought to its conclusion.

ADR ORGANISATIONS

The biggest hurdle to the use of ADR is very often persuading all the parties to a dispute to agree to participate. In the absence of a clause providing for ADR in a contract (see pages 58–59 below), the involvement of an independent ADR body can assist in convincing an unwilling party to participate.

Many of the major international and regional arbitration institutions have developed procedures to promote the resolution of disputes by ADR. For example, the ICC, the LCIA, the AAA/ICDR, the WIPO Arbitration and Mediation Centre and the HKIAC all offer ADR services, as does the CPR Institute for Dispute Resolution in New York. Each institution has a set of rules governing the relevant procedure and some may maintain lists of individuals from which the parties can select a neutral. Some of these rules are considered further below. ICSID also offers a conciliation procedure.

UNCITRAL has developed Conciliation Rules, aimed at providing parties with an internationally harmonised set of rules suited to international commercial disputes. UNCITRAL has also drawn up a Model Law on International Commercial Conciliation. Further reference is made to the UNCITRAL Conciliation Rules below.

In addition to the arbitration institutions, domestic organisations promoting the resolution of disputes by ADR and offering ADR facilities have been set up in some countries. The leading such organisation in the United Kingdom is the Centre for Effective Dispute Resolution (CEDR), based in London.

FORMS OF ADR

ADR procedures take many forms. This is because they have usually been fashioned to take account of the particular circumstances of the dispute in question. The most commonly encountered forms of ADR are described below, although there is no prescribed format for any of the processes. There is room for considerable flexibility within the framework of each of the procedures described below so the relevant ADR procedure may be tailored to suit the needs of the parties.

Mediation

Mediation is the most commonplace form of ADR. For many lawyers, it is synonymous with "conciliation". However, their separate descriptions, as set out in this chapter, do enjoy a considerable degree of general acceptance.

In a mediation, a neutral mediator (who is usually appointed by agreement between the parties) attempts to assist the disputing parties to negotiate a settlement. As part of the process, the mediator will discuss the strengths and weaknesses of each case and attempt to get the process of negotiation going. This may all take place in joint session or may be a combination of separate and joint sessions, as the parties wish.

Some mediators see their role as merely to facilitate negotiations, whilst others take a more evaluative approach. Either way, a mediator has no power to make any decision or impose a view on the parties and the parties will always retain their right to have the dispute determined by a judge or arbitration tribunal, if it cannot be resolved by mediation. This being the case, it is usual for parties to agree that the mediation and all discussions and information produced for the purposes of the mediation (other than materials already openly available) will be confidential and privileged from disclosure in subsequent proceedings.

Once parties have agreed to mediation, the usual preparations involve:

(a) agreeing the time, venue and length of the mediation;
(b) identifying and appointing the mediator;
(c) preparing and sending to the mediator and the other parties a brief summary of one's case and the main supporting documents; and
(d) identifying who will be one's representative at the mediation – this needs to be a person with full authority to settle. Whilst the parties' lawyers can, and usually do, attend and play a useful role in the mediation, the primary role is that of the client's representative.

It is common for the above matters to be set out in a mediation agreement. The mediation agreement may also make provision for payment of the mediator's fees, which are usually shared equally between the parties, and for recording any settlement that is reached at the mediation.

The mediation itself will usually involve an opening joint session chaired by the mediator, at which each of the parties will briefly summarise its case, followed by private sessions between each of the parties and the mediator. If agreement is reached, the terms agreed will normally be recorded in writing.

Reflecting the consensual nature of mediation, it is open to either party to withdraw from the mediation at any time.

Once it has been agreed that there will be a mediation, parties can either enlist the services of an ADR organisation to administer the mediation and/or to appoint a mediator, or they can organise the mediation themselves, adopting one of the model procedures available if they so wish. In the United Kingdom, CEDR publishes a model mediation procedure.

Of the major arbitration institutions which offer ADR facilities, the ICC's ADR Rules (which replaced the ICC Rules of Optional Conciliation) provide a framework for mediation and the LCIA has a mediation procedure, as do the AAA/ICDR and the HKIAC. The CPR Institute for Dispute Resolution also publishes a model mediation procedure.

A detailed commentary on the rules and model procedures of the various institutions is beyond the scope of this book. Suffice to say that each set of rules provides a framework within which the mediation can take place and broadly covers matters such as the appointment of a mediator, the conduct of the mediation, confidentiality, settlement agreements, termination of the mediation and fees. Some, such as the UNCITRAL Conciliation Rules and the ICC ADR Rules, go further and provide for the parties to cooperate in good faith with the mediator (see Article 11 of the UNCITRAL Conciliation Rules and Article 5(5) of the ICC ADR Rules).

Finally, whilst there is generally no rule against commencing arbitration or court proceedings before the termination of a mediation process, some rules do require the parties to refrain from doing so except to preserve their rights, for example in relation to an impending time-bar. See for example Article 16 of the UNCITRAL Conciliation Rules and ground rule 4(i) of the CPR

Model Mediation Procedure. By contrast, paragraph 14 of the CEDR Model Mediation Procedure and agreement expressly permits court proceedings or arbitration to be commenced notwithstanding the mediation.

A settlement reached by mediation will be binding on the parties. However, it should be noted that, unlike an arbitral award, such a settlement agreement is not subject to direct enforcement by the courts. It will therefore fall to be enforced in the same way as a contract. To circumvent the need for separate proceedings to be brought in the event of breach of the settlement agreement, there are two possible courses open to the parties. First, if an arbitration tribunal has already been appointed when the mediation takes place, the arbitrators could be asked to make a consent award reflecting the parties' agreement. This would then be subject to enforcement in the same way as an ordinary arbitral award (for example by virtue of the New York Convention). Alternatively, where there is an arbitration agreement between the parties, they could appoint the mediator as an arbitrator solely for the purpose of making a consent award based on the agreement. However, in some states there may be doubt as to the efficacy of such an approach. This is because, by definition, there would be no dispute between the parties at the time of appointment of the arbitrators.

Conciliation

Conciliation is similar to mediation, in that it involves a neutral third party assisting the parties to negotiate a settlement of their dispute. However, in a conciliation the conciliator will take a view on what would be fair to settle the dispute. That view will be put to the parties as a recommendation, which may be accepted by them or which may form the basis for further negotiations between them. The recommendation is not binding on the parties.

The term "conciliation" is often used interchangeably with that of "mediation". This is illustrated by the UNCITRAL Conciliation Rules, whose ambit is, in fact, wider than their title suggests: they cover various procedures involving the use of an independent third party to assist settlement. The UNCITRAL Model Law on International Commercial Conciliation defines "conciliation" as "a process, whether referred to by the expression conciliation, mediation or an expression of similar import, whereby parties request a third person ... to assist them ... to reach an amicable settlement".

Med-arb

Med-arb is an abbreviation for "mediation-arbitration". In med-arb, the parties initially attempt to resolve their dispute through mediation. If no agreement is reached, the parties refer the dispute to arbitration. Whilst this sequence of dispute resolution processes may be prescribed by a multi-tiered dispute resolution clause, what distinguishes mediation-arbitration as an ADR process in itself is the fact that the mediator and the arbitrator may be the same person. Note that this should not be confused with the situation where a mediator is appointed arbitrator solely for the purpose of making a consent award to make a settlement agreement immediately enforceable (as described above, and subject to the caution there expressed).

There is considerable debate as to whether the mediator should assume the role of arbitrator in the same case. There are several reasons for this:

(a) In the course of the mediation, the mediator will typically have received information in confidence from each of the parties separately. The information cannot be used by the mediator in the role as arbitrator as the mediation was conducted without prejudice, i.e. in a privileged context. However, it may be difficult for the mediator/arbitrator to disregard such information when making an award.

(b) The generally accepted view is that an arbitrator should not have discussions about the merits of the case with the parties separately, without notice being given to the other parties. A breach of this principle may, under normal circumstances, constitute a failure by the arbitrator to act fairly and impartially. Many legal systems impose a duty on arbitrators to act fairly and impartially, for example section 33 of the English Arbitration Act 1996. Article 18 of the UNCITRAL Model Law on International Commercial Arbitration requires the parties to be treated equally and Article 24(3) requires all documents and information provided to the arbitrator by one party to be divulged to the other party. By contrast, the private discussions between each party (separately) and the mediator typically represents a fundamental part of the mediation process itself.

(c) If the mediator adopted an evaluative approach in the mediation and expressed views as to the merits of the parties' respective cases, this may disqualify the mediator from acting as an arbitrator in the same case.

Another criticism of the med-arb process is that the assumption of this dual role by one individual may have an adverse effect on the mediation: the parties may be less open and forthcoming with the mediator because they know that the mediator may turn into an arbitrator, who will make a binding decision on the case.

As a safeguard against the above issues, the rules of some arbitration/ADR organisations provide that a mediator cannot act as an arbitrator in the same case without the written consent of all parties. See, for example, paragraph 19 of CEDR's Model Mediation Procedure and Agreement; Article 7(3) of the ICC ADR Rules; ground rule 4(k) of the CPR Institute for Dispute Resolution's Model Mediation Procedure; rule 21 of the HKIAC's Mediation Rules; and Article 19 of the UNCITRAL Conciliation Rules.

Notwithstanding the apparent conflict between the two elements of the med-arb process, it has apparently been used successfully in the United States and is regarded as an acceptable procedure in China. Furthermore, some countries and states have enacted legislation to permit an arbitrator to act as a mediator. See for example section 27(1)(b) of the New South Wales Commercial Arbitration Act 1984 and section 17(1) of the Singapore International Commercial Arbitration Act 2001.

There are plainly less objections to reversal of this process: that is, that an arbitrator ceases to act as such and by agreement of the parties is appointed mediator to facilitate a settlement of the dispute between them.

Mini-trial

Also known as "executive tribunal", this is a two-stage process which follows the form of a trial or arbitration (hence the term "mini-trial"). The first stage involves the parties' representatives making a presentation of their party's case to a panel which is usually made up of a senior executive from each party (having the power to commit the party to a settlement agreement) and usually chaired by a neutral third party. Each party may call witnesses and experts and the third party neutral may ask questions of witnesses during evidence and of the parties' lawyers during evidence and submissions.

The object of the exercise is to provide the executives with a brief overview of what both parties regard as the most important parts of their case and the weaknesses of their opponent's case. (The weaknesses of a party's case may previously have been withheld from its senior executives by staff wishing to protect their own positions or that of their subordinates.)

After the closing submissions, in the second stage of the process, the executives will retire with the neutral to consider the issues raised. They can form their own views as to the merits of the dispute, divorced from the emotions of those so far involved in the dispute, and proceed with negotiations for settlement on the basis of them.

The entire process is without prejudice and all information exchanged is confidential and is privileged from disclosure if the dispute proceeds to litigation or arbitration. The outcome of the mini-trial is not binding on any of the parties unless a settlement agreement is executed.

As with other ADR procedures, the mini-trial is a flexible process which can be adapted to suit the circumstances of each particular dispute. In some cases, it may be appropriate to combine features of mediation and mini-trial, so that the third party neutral "mediates" between the parties' executives to facilitate negotiations. Whatever format is used, the details should be set out in a written agreement between the parties and the neutral.

Guidance and model procedures and agreements for the mini-trial procedure are provided by ADR organisations such as CPR Institute for Dispute Resolution and CEDR. The ICC ADR Rules also provide for the use of the mini-trial as a settlement technique.

Neutral evaluation and expert determination

Neutral evaluation and expert determination are both processes whereby an independent third party is appointed to provide an opinion of the merits of the issues. The third party will usually be someone with expertise in the relevant field. Both processes are suitable where there is a need for a determination on a technical, scientific, legal or other specialist issue.

The key difference between the two processes lies in the status of the neutral's opinion. In an expert determination, the opinion of the expert is binding on the parties, with no right of appeal (except where the expert has decided on the wrong issue). In a neutral evaluation, the evaluator's opinion is not binding, the object of the exercise being to provide the parties with a realistic assessment of the strengths and weaknesses of their cases, thus providing a platform for a negotiated settlement. If only specific issues are referred to neutral evaluation or expert determination, the neutral's opinion may serve to narrow the issues in an existing or pending arbitration at an early stage.

Once a neutral has been appointed by the parties and terms of reference have been agreed, the parties will often provide the neutral with relevant documents and written statements to enable assessment of the issues in dispute and the relative strengths and weaknesses of each party's position. There may be a short meeting at which each party has an opportunity to provide the neutral with a brief summary of its case. In some cases, however, the parties may decide to dispense with a meeting and provide written statements only. The neutral will usually give an opinion in writing, the parties having agreed beforehand whether or not the neutral should give reasons with the opinion. All of these matters should be set out in an agreement between the parties and the neutral. Organisations such as CEDR can assist with standard form agreements.

As with other ADR procedures, the parties may opt to organise the neutral evaluation or expert determination themselves. Alternatively, they may have recourse to a specialist organisation for assistance in setting up the process and appointing a neutral. Such organisations can also provide guidance as to the suitability of a particular case or issue for these methods of ADR. In the United Kingdom, CEDR provides neutral evaluation and expert determination services. In addition, the ICC offers neutral evaluation under its ADR Rules and also has Rules for Expertise, which were revised in January 2003. In both ICC procedures, the opinion of the neutral/expert is non-binding, through the parties may agree that it is to be binding. It is worth noting that where the ICC's Rules of Expertise are used, the expert may proceed to produce a report even if one of the parties refuses to participate in the process, as long as that party has been given an opportunity to participate (Article 13(1)). Furthermore, whilst information given to the expert during the process is confidential, the expert's report will be admissible in any related arbitration, unless the parties agree otherwise (Article 12(4)).

Other forms of ADR

Other forms of ADR include the following.

(a) *Adjudication*: This is an interim dispute resolution method which is increasingly used in construction disputes. The adjudication process resembles a very fast track short form arbitration, though the result is only interim. The adjudicator gives a decision, in writing, which is binding until final determination by arbitration or agreement, thus enabling a construction project to proceed with the minimum of delay. The process is quick, informal and cheaper than court or arbitration proceedings. It has been made mandatory by legislation in several states.

(b) *Final offer arbitration*: This process involves the parties submitting to a neutral third party an offer setting out the terms on which they are prepared to settle. The neutral then chooses one of the parties' offers. Neither party should make an unrealistic offer as this might encourage the neutral to choose the opponent's offer.

(c) *Dispute review board (DB)*: The additional emphasis in this form of ADR is on the prevention of disputes. It has been developed for use primarily in the construction industry. A DB is an independent panel of individuals, appointed by the parties. The DB is kept informed about the status of the project. If a dispute arises, the idea is that the DB will make recommendations for its resolution. Whilst the recommendations are not binding, they usually have effect until the end of the project and they are admissible as evidence in later proceedings. The ICC published Rules for DB procedures in 2004.

SELECTING A NEUTRAL

Once the parties have agreed to participate in an ADR process, one of the first matters that they will have to agree is the appointment of a neutral. Just as the composition of an arbitral tribunal has a major influence on the conduct and even the outcome of an arbitration, so the identity of the neutral appointed for an ADR process is crucial to its success.

The qualities required in a neutral will depend on the ADR process and the particular circumstances of the dispute in question. However, in all cases experience of the ADR process concerned is an essential qualification as this, backed up by reliable feedback on the neutral's past performances, will be a demonstration of competence as a neutral.

Whether or not the neutral needs to have experience of the subject-matter of the dispute is more open to debate. Subject-related qualifications and experience may be more important if the neutral has to give an opinion, whether binding (as in expert determination or adjudication) or non-binding (as in conciliation or neutral evaluation). If the neutral's role is just facilitative, as in mediation, there is not necessarily any need to have experience of the subject matter, although in some cases it may help in engendering trust or confidence on the part of one or more of the parties.

The neutral should be impartial and should not give the appearance of bias. Where the ADR process is being organised through an institution, the neutral will be required to abide by that institution's code of conduct. For example, CEDR's neutrals act in accordance with CEDR's Code of Conduct and neutrals appointed under the ICC's ADR Rules or Rules of Expertise must, like ICC arbitrators, sign a statement of independence. Even where the parties are organising the ADR process themselves, the neutral may follow the code of conduct of a particular organisation or the parties may require the neutral to follow a particular code of conduct. In either case, this may be written into the ADR agreement between the parties and the neutral.

Other qualities to look for in a neutral include the following.

(a) Communication skills: The neutral must be a good communicator, given that the role includes persuading the parties to engage in the process and effectively liaising between the parties.

(b) Assertiveness: The neutral must be able to control the process and handle a potentially tense situation.

(c) Creative or lateral thinking: The success of an ADR process such as mediation or conciliation may depend on the neutral being able to think of an option for settlement which the parties may not have considered.

ADR CLAUSES

Because ADR can lead to the early resolution of a dispute, it is worth considering including in the parties' contract, at the time it is being negotiated, provision for ADR to take place prior to the commencement of legal proceedings or arbitration. A multi-tiered dispute resolution clause (also known as a "cascading" or "escalating" clause) provides for a tiered dispute resolution procedure, requiring attempts to be made to resolve disputes by successive methods, culminating in arbitration or court proceedings as a last resort. The merit of such clauses is that they allow a systematic process of negotiation with the opportunity of preserving the parties' relationship, rather than proceeding immediately to arbitration (which may have a negative effect on the relationship of the parties).

A basic clause may simply require the parties in the first instance to attempt to negotiate a settlement, failing which a reference should be made to arbitration. More complicated clauses might require a reference to designated representatives, then adjudication, then mediation and finally arbitration.

There is, unfortunately, insufficient space in this book to discuss in detail the drafting of an ADR or multi-tiered dispute resolution clause. However, some of the issues that should be considered when drafting are discussed below.

Enforceability of the dispute resolution clause

The issue here is whether each stage of the dispute resolution procedure is enforceable, i.e. will the courts prevent a claimant from pursuing legal proceedings or arbitration until they have exhausted the preceding steps to which they had agreed? Specifically, where the clause provides for negotiation and/ or mediation, is the agreement to negotiate or mediate enforceable? Both processes being consensual in nature and requiring the cooperation of the parties, the argument is that a party cannot be forced to engage in either process.

Whether or not each stage of the dispute resolution procedure is enforceable will depend on the law governing the dispute resolution clause and/or the law of the country in which it is sought to enforce the clause. A definitive answer cannot therefore be given here. However, a brief summary of the approach taken in some jurisdictions is given below. This indicates a measure of consistency of approach but if clarification on the position in a particular jurisdiction is required, advice should be taken from lawyers with expertise in that jurisdiction.

Under English law a bare agreement to negotiate is usually not enforceable but the courts recently enforced an agreement to mediate, staying court proceedings so that the dispute could be referred to mediation (*Cable & Wireless* v. *IBM UK Ltd* (2002)). In doing so, the judge treated the agreement to mediate as analogous to an arbitration agreement, which would have been enforceable by virtue of section 9 of the English Arbitration Act 1996. The reference in the dispute resolution clause to a specific mediation procedure was a factor which influenced the judge's decision.

A similar approach has been adopted by the Australian courts, which have enforced an agreement to conciliate which was sufficiently certain (*Hooper Bailie Associates Ltd* v. *Natcon Group Pty Ltd* (1992) (Supreme Court of New South Wales)) and refused to enforce an agreement to mediate which did not specify a procedure for the mediation (*Elizabeth Bay Developments Pty Ltd* v. *Boral Building Services Pty Ltd* (1995) (Supreme Court of New South Wales)). See also *Aiton Australia Pty Ltd* v. *Transfield Pty Ltd* (1999), where the Supreme Court of New South Wales held that an agreement to negotiate may be enforceable where it forms part of a broader dispute resolution process and where the process is defined with sufficient certainty.

Likewise, the French Cour de Cassation (Court of Appeal) in *Poiré* v. *Tripier* (14 February 2003) held that a clause requiring the parties to mediate before having recourse to legal proceedings was binding and that the courts must enforce such a clause if either of the parties relies on it. Interestingly, rather than staying the proceedings to enable a mediation to take place, the Cour de Cassation declared the legal action to be inadmissible and thereby effectively dismissed it.

In the United States, the New York courts have enforced an ADR clause by finding that the ADR procedure concerned constituted an arbitration for the purposes of section 2 of the Federal Arbitration Act. This provides that a written agreement to arbitrate is enforceable. In *AMF Inc.* v. *Brunswick Corp.* (1985) the parties agreed to submit future disputes to an "advisory third party", whose opinion would "not be binding upon the parties, but shall be advisory only". When a dispute arose, AMF invoked the "advisory third party" procedure but Brunswick refused to comply. AMF sought to compel Brunswick to submit to what it called a non-binding arbitration. In agreeing that the submission to the advisory third party fell within the definition of an arbitration in section 2 of the Federal Arbitration Act, the court found that, although the decision of the third party was to be non-binding, it would effectively settle the case.

Enforceability of an arbitration award

The issue here is whether a multi-tiered dispute resolution clause constitutes an arbitration agreement for the purpose of laws and conventions providing for enforcement of arbitration agreements, such as the New York Convention. It could be argued that a multi-tiered dispute resolution clause is not an agreement in writing under which the parties have undertaken to submit disputes to arbitration, within the meaning of Article II(1) of the New York Convention; it is an agreement whereby the parties agree only to resort to arbitration if they cannot resolve their dispute by the other prescribed methods. This argument may have some force if the pre-arbitral dispute resolution stages had not been exhausted when the reference to arbitration was made. However, an argument that the clause does constitute an arbitration agreement for these purposes is stronger if the parties exhausted the prescribed pre-arbitral stages before commencing arbitration proceedings.

Other issues

Some other issues which should be considered are as follows.

(a) It is important that each stage in the dispute resolution process is described with sufficient clarity, including who is to participate in that stage and when each stage has been exhausted. Time limits should be set for each step in the relevant procedure. Lack of clarity could result in a subsequent reference to arbitration being challenged on the ground that it was premature.

(b) There may be a concern that any arbitration may be time-barred by the time the agreed ADR procedure has been pursued. In *Poiré* v. *Tripier* (2003) the French Cour de Cassation held, *obiter dictum*, that the implementation of a mediation clause suspends the limitation period. In the absence of legislation or binding case law in the relevant jurisdiction, however, an obvious way to avoid limitation problems is to make appropriate provision in the dispute resolution clause. One solution might be to specify that the commencement of an ADR procedure suspends the limitation period until the procedure has been completed (which should in turn be defined). Alternatively, the parties may consider providing that, for time limitation purposes, the commencement of the first stage in the dispute resolution procedure should be regarded as the date on which the arbitration was commenced. If the latter solution is adopted, it is important to specify that this concession is for limitation purposes only. Otherwise, the parties risk losing the right to object to issues such as the substantive jurisdiction of the arbitrators if an arbitration ultimately ensues (see, for example, section 73 of the English Arbitration Act 1996, which provides that the right to object may be lost if not exercised forthwith or within the relevant time limit). In the absence of provision in the dispute resolution clause, a standstill agreement, suspending the limitation period during the ADR phase, may be appropriate.

(c) The parties may wish to reserve the right to have recourse to the courts to seek interim relief, without prejudice to the procedure set out in the dispute resolution clause.

(d) Problems may also arise when the nature or scope of disputes changes during the process. For example, there may be a new dispute arising from the treatment of the original dispute in an earlier tier, or step in the process. Care needs to be taken to avoid an infinite regression back to the first step of the process each time a new dispute arises out of the process itself.

Drafting ADR or multi-tiered dispute resolution clauses

Assistance in drafting ADR or multi-tiered dispute resolution clauses may be obtained from the following:

(a) the arbitration institutions, such as the ICC, the LCIA and the AAA/ICDR; or

(b) organisations such as:
  (i) CPR Institute for Dispute Resolution in New York;
  (ii) CEDR in London;
  (iii) the Australian Commercial Disputes Centre in Sydney; or
  (iv) the HKIAC.

It may be worth checking to see if a particular institution has a suggested multi-tiered dispute resolution clause if the parties are proposing to opt for arbitration administered by that institution. Interesting differences can be seen in the effects of respective suggested clauses for multi-tiered mediation followed by arbitration, published by the ICC and the LCIA.

CHAPTER 5

THE COMMENCEMENT OF THE ARBITRATION AND THE APPOINTMENT OF THE ARBITRAL TRIBUNAL

INTRODUCTION

The commencement of the arbitration and the appointment of the arbitral tribunal are dealt with together because they are usually very closely linked in most systems of arbitration law and in the rules of arbitration institutions. This is understandable: as a purely practical matter, an arbitration cannot progress very far without a tribunal to give directions for the further conduct of the proceedings.

The first part of this chapter will focus on the commencement of an arbitration, including a discussion of (a) the manner in which an arbitration is commenced and (b) time limits for commencing arbitration. The second part of the chapter will concentrate on issues relevant to the composition of the tribunal, such as the number of arbitrators, the method of appointment, matters to consider when selecting an arbitrator, the role of a party-nominated arbitrator and the removal of arbitrators.

PRELIMINARY MATTERS

When considering either the commencement of the arbitration or the appointment of the tribunal, the first thing to consider is the arbitration agreement. A properly drafted agreement for, or submission to, non-institutional arbitration should provide for the commencement of the arbitration and the composition of the tribunal, including how the tribunal is to be appointed. Where the arbitration agreement incorporates a set of rules (which is invariably the case in institutional arbitration and also where a non-institutional arbitration clause refers to the UNCITRAL Arbitration Rules or trade rules), such rules will normally contain provisions governing these matters.

Where there is nothing in the agreement or any such rules, there may be provision for making default appointments in the arbitration law of the country which is the seat of the arbitration and this should be checked in any event. In countries with a developed system of arbitration law (which obviously includes those jurisdictions which have adopted the UNCITRAL Model Law), the state arbitration law will contain provisions for the commencement of the arbitration and the composition and appointment of the tribunal. Such laws will also provide for the situation where an agreed mechanism for appointment has become inoperable because one of the parties refuses to co-operate, or where the appointing authority refuses to perform the appointment, has ceased to or never did exist, or is inadequately identified.

The arbitration proceedings themselves, at the time they are commenced, must have as their object the resolution of an existing dispute between the parties to the arbitration agreement. The particular dispute must also be arbitrable if it is to be the subject of an arbitration, as discussed on page 13 above.

As to whether there is a dispute, it was formerly the case in England that if a debt was unquestionably due, there was no "dispute" which could be referred to arbitration and the court would therefore refuse to stay proceedings before them in favour of arbitration. However, this is no longer the case and, in common with the arbitration laws of other countries, whether there is a "dispute" is a matter for the arbitral tribunal to decide. English courts have therefore ruled that, however indisputable the claimant's claim allegedly is, if a defendant does not admit liability there remains a "dispute" (*Halki Shipping Corp.* v. *Sopex Oils Ltd* (1997)).

THE COMMENCEMENT OF THE ARBITRATION

The manner in which an arbitration is formally commenced will depend upon the relevant arbitration rules and arbitration law of the seat. The extent to which modifications by the parties are permissible depends on the law of the seat and, in the case of institutional arbitration, also on the extent to which the rules permit or the institution is willing to accept departures from their norm. The following brief survey of institutional rules and arbitration laws provides examples of the various ways in which an arbitration may be commenced.

Applicable rules and laws

   (a) Institutional rules:

       (i) The ICC: by sending a Request for Arbitration to the ICC Court. Where a dispute is to be settled by three arbitrators, the request should contain the claimant's nomination of an arbitrator. The arbitration commences on the date the request is received by the ICC Court (Article 4).

      (ii) The LCIA: the procedure adds a requirement over and above those for the ICC, namely that the respondent must be sent a copy of the Request simultaneously (Article 1).

     (iii) The AAA/ICDR: by written notice to the AAA/ICDR and the other party, with the arbitration commencing on the date the notice is received by the AAA/ICDR. The notice may include proposals as to the means of designating and the number of arbitrators (Article 2).

(iv) CIETAC: by written Application for Arbitration sent to CIETAC, together with the prescribed fee (Article 14). The arbitration commences on the date CIETAC issues Notice of Arbitration (Article 13).

Generally speaking, it is one of the advantages of institutional arbitration that the risk of delayed service on the respondent is avoided.

(b) The UNCITRAL Arbitration Rules: by notice of arbitration given to the other party, with the arbitration commencing on the date the notice is received by that party. The notice shall include a proposal as to the number of arbitrators and may include the nomination of an arbitrator (Article 3).

(c) The UNCITRAL Model Law: by request for reference of the dispute to arbitration sent to the respondent. The arbitration commences on the date the request is received by the respondent (Article 21).

(d) State arbitration laws:

(i) England and Wales: unless otherwise agreed by the parties, by written notice (a) requiring the respondent to appoint an arbitrator or agree to the appointment of an arbitrator; (b) requiring the respondent to submit the dispute to a named arbitrator; or (c) where an appointment is to be made by a third party (e.g. an institution), by written notice to that person requesting them to make an appointment (section 14 of the Arbitration Act 1996).

(ii) Germany: unless otherwise agreed by the parties, by written notice containing the names of the parties, the matter in dispute and a reference to the arbitration agreement (§1044 of the German Code of Civil Procedure).

The general rule is that a notice of arbitration is effective when it is actually received by the respondent, so the date of receipt will be the decisive date for commencement. However, the relevant law should be checked carefully.

Time limits

The date of the commencement of an arbitration has more than just formal relevance, particularly when there is a possibility of a time-bar. Time limits for the bringing of claims in arbitration may take two forms:

(a) Contractual, i.e. where a time limit is contained in the parties' agreement. In a properly drafted agreement, the time limit should be capable of being precisely established. A very short contractual deadline which has been overlooked need not always be fatal: the law of some countries (including England) may permit time limits to be extended where undue hardship would otherwise be caused or may regard the time limit as invalid under the *lex causae* (e.g. as being an unfair contract term).

(b) Statutory, i.e. where the time limit is established by relevant legislation. The question is: which legislation applies? There are two possibilities: the law of the seat (the *lex arbitri*) or the law which is applicable to the substance of the dispute (the *lex causae*). Many states (notably those from the civil law tradition) treat time limits as matters of substance which will therefore be governed by the *lex causae*. Other states (especially common law jurisdictions) tend to regard time limits as procedural in nature and they will therefore be governed by the *lex arbitri*.

When the seat of an arbitration is in a state where limitation is regarded as a procedural matter, but the *lex causae* views time limits as substantive, a conflict may arise where the limitation period under the *lex arbitri* expires earlier than that under the *lex causae*. This will usually be resolved in favour of the *lex arbitri*. Where the shorter period is that of the *lex causae*, the claim will in any event be time-barred and the limitation provision of the *lex arbitri* will cease to be relevant.

If there is a possible limitation issue, a careful check should be made of the steps that need to be taken to commence proceedings within the time limit. This will depend upon whether the time limit is contractual or statutory. For instance, the contract might require a claimant to make a claim in writing and nominate its arbitrator within a certain period of time. In this case, the requirement is only complied with when the claimant has done both.

The position may be less straightforward where there is a statutory time limit. The relevant statute will usually provide that the commencement of the arbitration will stop time running and it may then specify the steps that constitute "commencement". It may be that those steps do not correspond with the requirements for commencing an arbitration set out in the rules of the chosen arbitration institution. For example, the statute might state that an arbitration commences with the service on the respondent of a notice to submit a dispute to a named arbitrator, whereas the rules of the parties' chosen institution might provide that the arbitration is commenced when the institution receives the request for arbitration. However, this need not be a problem. Provided that the statutory rule can be varied by the parties' agreement (the choice of the relevant institution by the parties constituting such agreement), the arbitration will have been commenced within the limitation period if the institution receives the request (together with anything else required by the rules, such as payment of a fee) on the last day of the limitation period. It is then irrelevant when the institution serves the request for arbitration on the respondent.

It is also important to consider carefully the way in which the claims are formulated in the initial request for arbitration. The request will, at least initially, define the scope of the claims actually brought in the arbitration. Only those claims set out in the request for arbitration will be considered to have been brought at the date of "commencement" for the purposes of any relevant limitation periods. Claims must be sufficiently described to ensure that they form a part of the arbitration in their entirety. Note also that there is a conceptual difference between common law systems, which typically define a claim by reference to a particular "cause" or "cause of action", and civil law systems, which define a claim by reference to the relief being sought on the basis of the facts asserted (e.g. the *Streitgegenstand* in German law).

THE APPOINTMENT OF THE TRIBUNAL

The number of arbitrators

The arbitration agreement should first be checked to see if the parties have specified the number of arbitrators. In theory, in the absence of any provision to the contrary in the law applicable to the arbitration agreement or in the rules applicable to the arbitration, there is no limit to the number of arbitrators which the parties may agree to include in the arbitral tribunal. In practice, however, most international commercial arbitrations are conducted before a tribunal of one or three arbitrators, a fact reflected in most sets of arbitral rules. Exceptionally, it may be appropriate for certain multi-party arbitrations to be conducted before a tribunal consisting of more than three arbitrators in order to ensure that all of the parties have an equal opportunity to participate in the appointment process (see pages 43–44 above), although there are other, more efficient ways of solving this problem (see page 44 above).

Where three arbitrators are appointed, one of them will be designated the chairman of the tribunal and may also be given authority to make directions for the conduct of the arbitration proceedings alone.

It is possible under some systems of law, and in certain trade arbitrations, to have a tribunal composed of two arbitrators, each party appointing one of them. In order to avoid deadlock, the arbitrators should have the power to appoint an umpire to settle the dispute. For most commercial arbitrations, however, two is an unsatisfactory number of arbitrators and some laws (e.g. the English Arbitration Act 1996) deem that an agreement to refer disputes to a two-party tribunal includes provision for the appointment of a chairman unless this is expressly excluded.

Where the parties fail to specify the number of arbitrators in their arbitration agreement, the provisions of any rules which have been incorporated into the agreement must be considered. For example, the rules of the AAA/ICDR, the ICC and the LCIA all provide that one arbitrator is to be appointed unless the relevant institution is of the view that the circumstances merit the appointment of a tribunal of three arbitrators. The UNCITRAL Arbitration Rules provide that there will be three arbitrators unless otherwise agreed.

If the relevant rules are silent or no rules have been incorporated into the arbitration agreement, the provisions of the law applicable to the arbitration proceedings should be checked. A significant factor here is the amount at stake in the dispute. English law specifies a single arbitrator unless the parties have agreed otherwise. Conversely, the UNCITRAL Model Law provides that there will be three arbitrators, unless the parties agree otherwise.

Matters to be taken into account when deciding on the number of arbitrators are set out at page 36 above.

The manner in which appointment of arbitrators may be made

The source for establishing the procedure for the appointment of the tribunal will again be the arbitration agreement, any relevant arbitration rules and the arbitration law of the seat.

There are three main routes by which a tribunal may be appointed: by agreement, by an appointing authority or by the state courts. As will be seen below, these routes need not be mutually exclusive and are often combined.

(a) *Agreement*: A number of techniques may be employed to assist the parties in reaching agreement on the composition of the arbitral tribunal, the most common of which is the exchange between the parties of lists of names of acceptable arbitrators. If the name of an arbitrator appears on both parties' lists, then that arbitrator will be appointed. (If two names are common to the lists, then the parties will have to reach agreement on one of them.) It frequently happens that there are no names common to the lists. That need not preclude the appointment of an arbitrator named on just one of the lists if the party naming that arbitrator can persuade the other party as to suitability.

In the case of a sole arbitrator, if the parties are unable to agree on an appointment, the arbitrator must be appointed by the chosen appointing institution (if any) or, failing that, the state court.

The parties should agree that, if they fail to come up with an acceptable name, any appointing authority subsequently requested to make an appointment should not be prevented from appointing an arbitrator named on one of the lists. If there is no such provision, the arbitrator best qualified to deal with the dispute might be excluded from the running, either because a party will not propose that name in the initial stages for fear of disqualifying the person later, or because the mere fact of being proposed by one party may act as a *de facto* disqualification for later appointment by an institution in the absence of agreement between the parties.

The procedure for the appointment of a three-arbitrator tribunal usually starts with the nomination of an arbitrator by each of the parties. The parties will often have agreed that the party-appointed arbitrators should choose a chairman, thus trying to ensure that the arbitrators appoint someone in whom they both have confidence and with whom they can work. Sometimes co-arbitrators also use the exchange of lists technique.

There are two further important points to consider in the context of the parties' agreement regarding the arbitral tribunal:

(i) It is both unwise and unusual (unless coupled with a detailed mechanism for what is to happen in default) to name a particular arbitrator in an agreement to submit future disputes to arbitration. The particular candidate may die or otherwise become unable or unwilling to act as arbitrator. It is, however, perfectly sensible to include the name of a mutually acceptable arbitrator in an agreement providing for the submission of an existing dispute to arbitration.

(ii) Some institutions, such as the ICC and the LCIA, retain the final say in the appointment of an arbitrator, even if the parties have agreed the nomination. This is to enable the institution to prevent an appointment which it believes would be inappropriate, for instance where it has evidence that the proposed arbitrator is not wholly independent of one of the parties.

(b) *Appointing authority*: The arbitration agreement may provide that the tribunal is to be appointed by a specific individual or body. Alternatively, it may provide for recourse to an appointing authority where the parties have been unable to agree on the composition of the arbitral tribunal or one of the parties has failed to nominate its arbitrator (where the tribunal is to be comprised of three arbitrators) within the agreed period of time. There is always a risk that one party may try to obstruct the proceedings by refusing to agree or nominate an arbitrator. It is therefore advisable to specify an appointing authority in the arbitration agreement, to save time and avoid problems later.

Where the arbitration is institutional, the institution will act as the appointing authority. Whilst most institutions maintain lists of arbitrators considered suitable for appointment, the ICC will refer to one of its National Committees, usually of the state of the party in default of making an appointment or, in the case of the appointment of a chairman, the state that is to be the seat of the arbitration.

Appointing authorities for non-institutional arbitrations may be chosen from one of the following.

(i) A trade association, where the contract relates to that particular trade.

(ii) The president for the time being of some professional institution connected in some way to the contract work. Thus, the President of the Institution of Civil Engineers may be called upon to nominate the arbitrator for a construction dispute in the United Kingdom.

(iii) Some arbitration institutions, such as the ICC, are also prepared to take on the limited role of appointment in a non-institutional arbitration not otherwise subject to its rules.

It is rare, and for good reason (such as the possibility of death or other intervening incapacity), to find a named individual specified as the appointing authority. For similar reasons, it is always important that the appointing authority, where it is not an individual, should be one which can be assured of continuing to be in existence through to the completion of the arbitration, bearing in mind that further appointments may have to be made if an arbitrator dies or is removed.

The UNCITRAL Rules provide a useful fall back provision where the parties have failed to specify an appointing authority, empowering the Secretary-General of the Permanent Court of Arbitration at The Hague to designate a suitable authority to undertake that role.

(c) *The state courts*: Where the parties have failed to appoint a complete tribunal and have not agreed on an appointing authority, the state courts may be called upon to make the necessary appointment or appointments. However, it is important to realise that the courts cannot always be relied upon to come to the rescue. First of all, a state court must have jurisdiction before it can do so. Its jurisdiction will usually be limited to those arbitrations with a specified seat within its jurisdiction or where the dispute is governed by its law. The court must also have been granted the function of appointment by the arbitration law.

Whilst the courts of most states which have an effective system of arbitration law will have been given a power of appointment, establishing the court's jurisdiction may be more problematic: a badly drafted arbitration clause which fails to specify an appointing authority may also fail to specify the seat of the arbitration. If so, and if there is no other indication of where the parties intended that the arbitration should take place, it may be difficult to persuade a court that it has jurisdiction to exercise its powers of appointment.

The appointment process will not end until all of the members of the tribunal have accepted their appointment and (in the case of some institutional rules) the institution has approved the appointment.

Selecting an arbitrator

The criteria for selecting an arbitrator will depend to a certain extent on whether the arbitrator is being selected as a sole arbitrator or as the party-nominated arbitrator for a tribunal of three arbitrators. In addition to the criteria set out below, the requirements of the parties' agreement, any relevant institutional rules and the mandatory rules of law of the seat of the arbitration are also important. For example:

(a) The parties may have agreed that the arbitrator should have a particular qualification or experience relevant to the subject matter of their dispute.

(b) Arbitration institutions endeavour to pre-empt allegations of bias and partiality by imposing restrictions on the nationality of the arbitrator to be selected. Both the ICC and the LCIA Arbitration Rules provide that, when appointing a sole arbitrator or chairman, the appointee is not to be of the same nationality as any of the parties. (The situation is, of course, different if both parties have the same nationality.) The UNCITRAL Arbitration Rules also encourage this approach.

(c) Some state laws stipulate mandatory requirements, particularly in relation to nationality.

An important aspect of selection of the tribunal is that any chosen arbitrator should be competent, both by training and experience, to deal with the particular issues that will arise in the arbitration. International commercial arbitration can throw up a number of "legal" issues, derived both from the various systems of law which may be applicable to different aspects of the arbitration and from the problem of determining which law may be applicable. Accordingly, where an arbitrator is to be a sole arbitrator, a person with a legal background and, preferably, experience in international arbitration will probably be the most appropriate choice. The same reasons favour the appointment of someone with a similar background as chairman of a tribunal of three arbitrators, especially as the chairman will often be empowered to make procedural decisions alone.

It is not necessary for party-appointed arbitrators to have a legal background unless the dispute is of a particularly legal nature. On the contrary, it is one of the advantages of submitting a dispute to arbitration that it can be adjudicated upon by anyone with knowledge of the relevant industry. Thus, engineers and architects are sometimes appointed to deal with construction disputes. Some such arbitrators go on to acquire considerable expertise in the law and practice of arbitration. Parties are, however, often reluctant that their appointee should be the only arbitrator on the tribunal without a legal background if both the other appointments are, or are likely to be, lawyers.

Whatever the background of the members of the tribunal, it is essential that those selected should be:

(a) available, otherwise hearings will be delayed interminably. Famous names in any particular field frequently have very full diaries;

(b) fluent in the language of the arbitration;

(c) independent and impartial. These requirements are discussed at page 85 below. Institutions typically require arbitrators to complete a declaration of independence before taking up an appointment. An arbitrator who becomes aware of any fact which might put his independence and impartiality in doubt is under an obligation to bring it to the attention of the parties. Disclosure of such a fact does not automatically disqualify an arbitrator. In 2004 the IBA published *Guidelines on Conflicts of Interest in International Arbitration* (see page 85 below). The Guidelines establish general principles, and give examples, of what will and will not disqualify an arbitrator.

THE ROLE OF A PARTY-NOMINATED ARBITRATOR

Discussion of the independence and the impartiality of the arbitrator inevitably leads to consideration of the role of a party-nominated arbitrator and what a party may legitimately expect of such an arbitrator. In most jurisdictions today a party-nominated arbitrator is not the representative or advocate of the nominating party and may not accept instructions from or communicate directly with that party alone once appointed.

THE TRIBUNAL'S FEES AND EXPENSES

Establishing the entitlement to fees and expenses

The appointment of an arbitrator is not complete until it has been accepted by the arbitrator. Before accepting an appointment, an arbitrator will want to be satisfied as to the proposed remuneration. The parties too will want to know what level of fees the arbitrator will expect.

An arbitrator's remuneration, and the manner in which it is fixed and paid, depends largely on the character and standing of the arbitrator, the nature of the arbitration and, in particular, on whether the arbitration is institutional or non-institutional.

(a) *Institutional arbitration*: fees are negotiated or fixed by the institution. The way in which the various institutions set about doing this varies considerably. For example:

  (i) The AAA/ICDR will attempt to broker an appropriate hourly or daily rate between the parties and the arbitrator, which will take into account the size and complexity of the case, failing which it will establish an appropriate rate.

  (ii) The ICC does not fix the fees at the outset. Instead, fees are to be fixed within a range which is established by reference to the amount in dispute. (This has the advantage that it discourages the parties from making inflated claims.) The point within the range at which the fees will be fixed is influenced by the time spent on the case and its complexity. In exceptional cases the ICC may fix fees outside the range.

  (iii) The LCIA fixes fees by reference to a daily or hourly rate for the time spent by the arbitrator. The rate is established and is notified to the parties at the time the tribunal is appointed, though it may be revised if the arbitration is particularly long running. The rate will be influenced by the complexity of the dispute and the particular qualifications of the arbitrator.

(b) *Non-institutional arbitration*: If nothing is agreed about fees, an arbitrator is usually entitled to a "reasonable" fee. What is "reasonable" may vary considerably, depending on the standpoint from which it is viewed. To avoid later argument, fees should be agreed at the time of appointment. (An exception to this may be where the dispute arises in connection with a trade which has an established customary basis for remunerating arbitrators.) The most common method of remuneration is by reference to a daily or hourly rate for time spent, but fees may be agreed on the basis of the amount in dispute or any other basis the parties consider appropriate.

The expenses incurred by the arbitrator in the course of the arbitration may also be reimbursed. These are usually recovered on the basis of an account prepared by the arbitrator. The parties may, however, agree to simplify matters (where, for example, the arbitrator has to stay away from home for the duration of the hearing) by giving the arbitrator an agreed daily or weekly amount out of which expenses are to be met.

Unless dealt with carefully, the arbitrator's fees can be the source of difficulty and embarrassment, for example in the following situations:

(a) Where one party is unhappy with the level of fees being demanded. A party may quite legitimately feel that the fees being requested are excessive, but feel embarrassed about negotiating with the arbitrator for fear that the arbitrator will thereby become prejudiced against that party in the proceedings. This highlights the importance of the following:
   (i) agreeing, if possible, a common approach on fees with the other party before any negotiations are commenced with the arbitrator;
   (ii) ensuring that negotiations are conducted in the presence of representatives of both parties.

(b) *Cancellation*: In any substantial arbitration there is the possibility of lengthy hearings. Dates for the hearings have to be fixed and time set aside in arbitrators' diaries. If a case settles shortly before a hearing, the arbitrators may find themselves with a shortage of work over the period of time that they had set aside for the hearing. To protect themselves against this, some arbitrators ask the parties to agree to a cancellation fee, usually on a sliding scale which increases as cancellation gets closer to the hearing date. There is nothing improper in this, though the law of some countries requires that the arbitrator must have reserved the right to a cancellation fee at the time of appointment. The terms of the London Maritime Arbitrators' Association specifically provide for a cancellation fee. In order to avoid any suggestion of misconduct on the part of the arbitrator, the cancellation fee should be negotiated with the parties together.

   Institutions such as the ICC will not permit arbitrators to enter into agreements for cancellation fees, but will take the fact of late cancellation into account when fixing the arbitrators' fees.

(c) Where members of a three-person tribunal come from different jurisdictions with widely differing scales of remuneration for legal services and the parties have agreed substantially different rates of remuneration for their appointees. This problem is avoided in institutional arbitration, where the remuneration is fixed by the institution.

Securing payment of the tribunal's fees and expenses

A degree of security is afforded to the tribunal by the fact that it is generally not obliged to publish its award (i.e. deliver it to the parties) until such time as its fees have been paid. However, many arbitrations settle prior to the making of an award. Unless the tribunal's fees and expenses are secured in some way, it could be left without payment.

In the case of non-institutional arbitrations, the tribunal will usually require the parties to provide a deposit to secure its fees. The deposit should be kept by the tribunal in a separate interest-bearing account. The tribunal may also agree to security being provided by way of bank guarantee.

Arbitration institutions such as the AAA/ICDR, the ICC and the LCIA have rules governing the provision of deposits as security for the tribunal's costs.

The usual practice is to require the parties to pay the deposit in equal amounts. If the respondent refuses to pay its share of the deposit, the arbitration is unlikely to proceed, unless the claimant pays the respondent's share as well. This is not quite as onerous as it seems because the amount of the additional payment can be dealt with in the award and thus recovered by the claimant (on the assumption that the claimant wins and that the respondent has assets to meet the award). In addition, the claimant might ask the tribunal for an interim injunction compelling the respondent to pay his share of the advance. The respondent's refusal to pay its share amounts to a breach of the arbitration agreement, which might later be used against it if the claimant brings court proceedings and the respondent seeks to rely on the arbitration agreement.

REMOVAL OF ARBITRATORS

Having accepted an appointment, an arbitrator is thereafter generally under a duty to conduct the arbitration with reasonable diligence through to its conclusion in an award, unless both parties have decided in the meantime that the arbitrator should be replaced. An objection to the appointment and a demand for the removal of the arbitrator may be made by one of the parties alone.

The matters which are important in the context of removal will be identified in the rules governing the arbitration or, where silent, in the law of the country where the arbitration takes place. They usually include the matters set out in the following section.

Circumstances in which removal may be appropriate

An arbitrator may be removed for the following principal reasons:

(a) where there are justifiable doubts as to the arbitrator's impartiality or independence;

(b) where the arbitrator lacks the qualifications which the parties have agreed to be necessary in their submission to arbitration; and/or

(c) where the arbitrator is prevented from fulfilling his functions (e.g. by illness), or is not fulfilling them with reasonable diligence and in accordance with the rules governing the arbitration.

Applications for removal

Depending on the type of arbitration, an application for removal may be dealt with in the following ways.

(a) *Institutional arbitrations*: Applications are usually dealt with by the principal administrative organ of the institution (for example, the ICC International Court of Arbitration or the LCIA Court). The application may be made by one of the parties (or, in the case of the LCIA, by the remaining arbitrators) and must be made within the prescribed time limit or the party will be deemed to have waived its right to object. Time limits for many institutions are short—sometimes as little as 15 days from the date the party became aware of the circumstances upon which the application is based.

  A number of institutions provide that their decisions on such applications are to be regarded as final. This should nevertheless be viewed as subject to any mandatory provisions of the arbitration law of the seat, which may permit a further application to be made to the state courts. If the law of the seat does not support an application to the state courts, the participation of a biased or otherwise disqualified arbitrator can be a ground to oppose a motion to declare the award enforceable.

(b) *Non-institutional arbitrations*: Applications for removal of an arbitrator are usually made in the first instance to the tribunal itself. If unsuccessful, a further application can generally be made to the state courts at the seat of the arbitration. In the case of non-institutional arbitrations conducted in accordance with the UNCITRAL Arbitration Rules, if a decision has to be made on an application to remove an arbitrator, it will be made by the authority with power to appoint arbitrators designated pursuant to the rules.

The consequences of removal

When an arbitrator is removed, a vacancy is created which must normally be filled before the arbitration proceedings can continue. A vacancy may also be created when an arbitrator dies, resigns or refuses to participate further in the arbitration proceedings. The vacancy will usually be filled by an appointment made in the same manner as that in which the original appointment was made. When that is no longer possible (as, for example, when arbitrators have agreed on a chairman, but cannot agree on who is to fill the vacancy left on the chairman's removal), the procedure set out in any relevant rules must be followed. In non-institutional arbitrations the courts of the seat of the arbitration may act on an application made by one of the parties to fill the vacancy, provided that they have power under their law to do so.

Any incoming arbitrator must have an opportunity to become acquainted with the parties' submissions and evidence. If a replacement takes place after a hearing has commenced, the hearing will usually have to be halted to enable the arbitrator to read the relevant papers. The parties may agree that the hearing need not be repeated, particularly where a transcript of the hearing has been made and can be read by the incoming arbitrator.

Where hearings are likely to be lengthy and an arbitrator is elderly, it is common to insure the life of the arbitrator so that, if the arbitrator dies before signature of the award, the additional costs in the arbitration arising out of the death may be recovered.

Very occasionally, a party-nominated arbitrator refuses to take an active part in the arbitration proceedings at a very late stage in order to try to frustrate an award adverse to the party which appointed that arbitrator. In these circumstances, the expense and delay which would otherwise be occasioned by appointing a replacement arbitrator may sometimes be avoided by continuing the proceedings before a "truncated" tribunal consisting of the remaining arbitrators. Article 11(1) of the AAA/ICDR's International Arbitration Rules makes specific provision for this, as do §1052 of the German Code of Civil Procedure and Article 31 of the UNCITRAL Model Law. The position may be more difficult if, instead of simply refusing to take part, the arbitrator resigns.

CHAPTER 6

THE JURISDICTION, POWERS AND OBLIGATIONS OF THE TRIBUNAL

INTRODUCTION

This chapter is concerned with the framework within which the arbitral tribunal is to act. It considers the jurisdiction of the tribunal (in particular, the nature and identity of the disputes upon which the tribunal may adjudicate) and goes on to cover what the tribunal should do, may do and should not do in the course of dealing with such disputes. It also reviews the courses open to a party which believes that the tribunal has exceeded its jurisdiction or failed to perform an obligation.

Applicable laws and rules

Once again, there are many provisions, rules and laws which might have to be considered. They should be considered in the order set out below, because it is one of the fundamental principles of international commercial arbitration that the will (i.e. agreement) of the parties should be paramount, subject to such limited restrictions as may be appropriate for reasons of public policy and which may be found in relevant applicable laws. These provisions, rules and laws include the following.

(a) In the first instance, the provisions of the parties' agreement to arbitrate. These are the primary source for establishing the jurisdiction of the tribunal (and the extent or "scope" of that jurisdiction) and may include express reference to powers and obligations to be conferred or imposed on the tribunal.

(b) Any arbitration rules (whether of an institution or the UNCITRAL Arbitration Rules) applicable to the proceedings. These may, for example, give the tribunal power to appoint experts, where the parties have not agreed on that. They may also require the tribunal to make its award within a specified period of time.

(c) The law applicable to the arbitration agreement. This may be relevant in the context of the arbitrability of disputes (see page 12 above), thus having a bearing on the jurisdiction of the tribunal.

(d) The law applicable to the arbitration proceedings themselves. This too may be relevant in the context of arbitrability. It may also be relevant in the context of filling gaps in the parties' agreement or in any applicable arbitration rules. Conversely, it may be important in imposing limitations on what the parties have otherwise agreed.

JURISDICTION

Introduction

Given the consensual nature of arbitration, it is clear that no one should be obliged to submit to arbitration without having agreed to it. Furthermore, having agreed to the arbitration of a particular dispute, a party to the arbitration should not have to acquiesce in the inclusion in the arbitration of further disputes which the other party may try to raise, but which are outside the scope of the parties' agreement. These latter disputes may be of a kind which the respondent party, for good reason, does not wish to have settled by arbitration.

The jurisdiction of a tribunal is usually considered from two viewpoints:

(a) Whether the tribunal has any jurisdiction at all. A tribunal will lack jurisdiction altogether if no enforceable arbitration agreement has been created. Factors preventing creation of such an agreement are dealt with at pages 25–27 above. A tribunal will also lack jurisdiction where the only matter in dispute between the parties does not fall within the scope of the arbitration agreement, or where some condition precedent to arbitration (such as obtaining a decision from the engineer in the case of certain construction disputes) has not been fulfilled at the time of the commencement of the arbitration.

(b) Whether the tribunal has jurisdiction over all of the disputes submitted to it, or only *some* of them. The answer to this question will be found by construing the arbitration agreement to determine what disputes the parties have agreed should be submitted to arbitration. Some of the matters which may give rise to difficulty in the context of establishing the scope of the tribunal's jurisdiction include the following.

   (i) The submission of claims founded in tort or delict together with claims founded in contract. An arbitration agreement that simply refers to "all claims arising under the contract" is likely (in some states at least) not to apply to claims founded in tort or delict.

  (ii) Disputes, not being all the disputes in the arbitration, which require some condition precedent to be fulfilled before they can be submitted to arbitration.

 (iii) Disputes arising after the commencement of the arbitration. These may fall outside the scope of the tribunal's jurisdiction if the jurisdiction is determined, and frozen, by the scope of the reference to arbitration as may be the case in an *ad hoc* arbitration.

 (iv) disputes existing at the time of the commencement of the arbitration which were not referred to in the original claim submission, but which the claimant subsequently attempts to introduce into the arbitration by way of amendment of its claim. Such disputes are usually within the scope of the tribunal's jurisdiction (though in the case of an ICC arbitration, in which terms of reference have been signed (as to which, see further on page 95), such amendments will not be permitted unless authorised by the tribunal (Article 19 of the ICC Arbitration Rules)).

In all of the cases referred to above any lack of jurisdiction can be cured by the parties agreeing that the tribunal is to have jurisdiction over the claims or disputes in question.

The consequences of absence of jurisdiction

If a tribunal lacks jurisdiction altogether, it has no authority to continue with the arbitration. If it does so, any award that it makes will be void and if a party attempts to rely on such an award, it will be set aside and enforcement refused.

Where the tribunal's lack of jurisdiction is only partial, the position is less straightforward. The tribunal clearly has jurisdiction to continue with the arbitration, but it should exclude from the proceedings those claims and disputes which are outside the scope of its jurisdiction. If the tribunal fails to do so, it runs the risk of having its award declared void, set aside and rendered unenforceable (see Article V(1)(c) of the New York Convention) in its entirety. Fortunately for the successful party in the arbitration, and depending on the law of the seat of the arbitration, this will not always be the case. The law of some countries, such as England, permits the court to set aside only that part of the award which has been made in excess of the tribunal's jurisdiction, provided that that part can be severed from the rest of the award. Where severance is not possible, the court may send back (or "remit", as it is often called) the award to the tribunal with a direction that it should make a proper award which excludes reference to claims or disputes which are outside the scope of the tribunal's jurisdiction. The proviso to Article V(1)(c) of the New York Convention also permits the severance of those parts of the award made in excess of the tribunal's jurisdiction.

What is a party to do if it believes that the tribunal lacks jurisdiction?

The most suitable course of action for a party which does not accept the jurisdiction of the tribunal turns partly on whether it is thought that the tribunal:

(a) has no jurisdiction at all; or
(b) does not have jurisdiction over all of the disputes submitted to it.

This division will therefore be used when considering possible courses of action below.

The following points must also be considered:

(a) The laws of many states give the tribunal power to deal with issues relating to both the existence and the scope of its own jurisdiction. Before acting, a check should be made for the existence of such a power. It is contained, for example, in:
   (i) Article 16 of the UNCITRAL Model Law;
   (ii) Article 1466 of the French Code of Civil Procedure;
   (iii) Article 1052 of the Netherlands Arbitration Act 1986.
(b) Subject to the laws applicable to the arbitration agreement and to the arbitration proceedings, the arbitration rules of many institutions (as well as the UNCITRAL Arbitration Rules) also give the tribunal power to deal with issues relating to both the existence and the scope of its own jurisdiction. See, for example:
   (i) Article 23 of the LCIA Arbitration Rules;
   (ii) Article 21 of the UNCITRAL Arbitration Rules; and
   (iii) Article 6 of the ICC Arbitration Rules.
(c) The rules and laws referred to above frequently impose time limits on the making of a challenge to the tribunal's jurisdiction. Thus, Article 16(2) of the UNCITRAL Model Law provides that a challenge shall be made not later than the submission of the defence. The existence of such a time limit may, however, not be effective in preventing a party from raising lack of jurisdiction as a defence to recognition or enforcement of the award, except, in the case of a partial challenge, where the court comes to the view that the party has waived the lack of jurisdiction.
(d) Whilst an arbitral tribunal generally has the power to decide on its own jurisdiction, that decision will seldom be final, in that:
   (i) the courts of the seat of the arbitration may set the decision aside; and
   (ii) the courts of the state where enforcement of an award is sought may refuse enforcement of an award if they are of the view that the tribunal did not have jurisdiction (Articles V(1)(a) and V(1)(c) of the New York Convention).

Partial challenge

A partial challenge to the jurisdiction of an arbitral tribunal is one that is limited to only some of the disputes submitted to the tribunal. It follows from the fact that the challenge is only partial that both parties accept that there is a valid arbitration agreement and a valid appointment of the tribunal. Accordingly, whilst a party which challenges the entire jurisdiction of the tribunal may have the option to ignore the arbitration proceedings altogether and to challenge any award when recognition and enforcement are sought, that is not a practical option where there is only a partial challenge. The tribunal may well write its award in a way in which the claims allegedly not within its jurisdiction are severable from the rest of the award, leaving at least that part of the award enforceable.

A party challenging the tribunal's jurisdiction as to some only of the disputes before it therefore has the following options.

(a) To apply to the tribunal in the course of the proceedings for a decision that it does not have jurisdiction with regard to the disputes said to be outside its jurisdiction. The tribunal will usually make a partial award on the application. Where the facts relevant to the issue of jurisdiction are closely connected with those relevant to the substance of the dispute (as where they concern the nature of the relief being claimed and whether or not such relief has been excluded by the agreement of the parties) the tribunal may refuse to make a partial award on jurisdiction, but leave the question of jurisdiction to be dealt with in its final award.

(b) To apply to the state courts at the seat of the arbitration (if the arbitration law of that state so allows) for:

    (i) a declaration that the arbitral tribunal does not have jurisdiction to deal with the claim in question; and/or

    (ii) if there is a suspicion that the tribunal will ignore the declaration, an injunction restraining the tribunal from continuing with the arbitration.

    Article 16(3) of the UNCITRAL Model Law requires that an application to the state courts to reverse the decision of the tribunal (made on an application under (a) above) must be made within 30 days of the tribunal's decision.

(c) To challenge the award in the courts of the state where it was made. Such a challenge must not be confused with an appeal on the merits of the dispute. It is an application to have the award declared void for having been made in excess of the tribunal's jurisdiction, and set aside. As indicated above, the state court may, where the good parts of the award are severable from those which are bad, decline to set the award aside, but will remit it to the tribunal with directions to make the award again without the offending parts. It may be tactically unwise for a party to use this option as its opening move in any challenge since, apart from any issues as to waiver, a court may not be well disposed toward a party which has let the arbitration run to an award (with all the expense that that involves) before raising the issue of jurisdiction.

(d) To resist the recognition and enforcement of the award in a foreign state (see Article V(1)(c) of the New York Convention) on the basis that it has been made in excess of the arbitral tribunal's jurisdiction. This may be a better course than (b) or (c) above where the state courts at the seat of the arbitration are mistrusted by the respondent.

The above options are not all mutually exclusive, although the laws of some countries do oblige a challenging party to make an application under (a) before an application under (b) is made.

Challenge to the entire jurisdiction

The most common ground for a challenge to the entire jurisdiction of the arbitral tribunal is the absence of a valid and enforceable arbitration agreement. This may be for any one or more of the reasons already discussed earlier (see pages 25–27 above). Other grounds include the following:

(a) the subject-matter of the dispute is not arbitrable under the law of the place of arbitration;

(b) the conditions precedent agreed upon by the parties for arbitration have not been fulfilled (for example, in certain construction disputes, the engineer's decision may not have been obtained);

(c) absence of a dispute (see page 62 above); or

(d) the entire dispute between the parties is not one which they have agreed should be submitted to arbitration.

Until relatively recently, and more particularly in common law states, a challenge to the entire jurisdiction of a tribunal gave rise to several conceptual difficulties, especially where the challenge was based on the absence altogether of a valid arbitration agreement. Those difficulties had as their origin the fact that the jurisdiction of the tribunal is derived from the agreement of the parties. The argument was that if there was no agreement, the tribunal could not have jurisdiction and the question was who could, and should, deal with the challenge.

As indicated above, the courts of most states do have jurisdiction to deal with any questions of jurisdiction arising in the course of an arbitration. However, parties usually agree to arbitration because they wish to avoid the involvement of the state courts and the publicity which might attach to it. Furthermore, there could be unnecessary delay to the progress of the arbitration whilst the court proceedings relevant to the issue of jurisdiction are completed. Finally, as explained at page 68 above, there could be difficulty in finding a state court prepared to accept jurisdiction over the matter (especially where the seat of the arbitration has not been established).

Asking the tribunal to deal with questions of jurisdiction would have prompted the objection that the tribunal had no authority to decide on jurisdiction, because the challenge was based on the fact that there was no valid arbitration agreement at all. Moreover, in the absence of an agreement, the tribunal itself had no legal standing and there was nothing to delineate its jurisdiction. The existence of this objection encouraged recalcitrant respondents to develop arguments with which to attack the validity of the arbitration agreement. One well-known and, on the face of it, reasonable assertion was that the arbitration clause contained in a commercial contract was an integral part of, and depended for its entire existence on, that contract and if that contract was invalid, or came to an end, the arbitration provision was likewise invalid or terminated. (We shall see below that such an assertion will not today find favour in most states.)

Faced with the possibility of increasing state court intervention in order to deal with issues related to jurisdiction, or, even worse, the neutralisation of an arbitration when no court could be found to intervene, arbitration practitioners found ways round the problems which have now received wide acceptance and which are recognised in the arbitration laws of many states and the rules of most arbitration institutions.

The most important of these was obtaining general acceptance of the existence of a arbitral tribunal's power (or "competence") to investigate and decide upon its own jurisdiction (or "competence", in the sense of "jurisdiction", thus giving rise to the expression "competence/competence" which is sometimes used to describe the power). If the tribunal decided that it had jurisdiction, it could continue with the arbitration, though the tribunal's decision could be overruled by a competent state court on an application made:

(a) immediately after the decision;
(b) after the award had been made; or
(c) when an attempt was made to have the award recognised or enforced in a foreign country.

This power is now to be found in:

(a) Article 16(1) of the UNCITRAL Model Law;
(b) Article 15(1) of the AAA/ICDR International Arbitration Rules;
(c) Article 6(2) of the ICC Arbitration Rules;
(d) Article 23(1) of the LCIA Arbitration Rules; and
(e) Article 21(2) of the UNCITRAL Arbitration Rules.

It may not, however, exist in all state arbitration laws. Therefore, in the case of non-institutional arbitration, the relevant state law must be checked for the existence, or otherwise, of the power. This is particularly important if the state law in question has not adopted the UNCITRAL Model Law. China, for example, has not adopted the UNCITRAL Model Law. Under Chinese law, a tribunal does not have the power to decide upon its own jurisdiction.

Another significant step was the reinforcement of the authority of the arbitral tribunal by recognising that an arbitration agreement contained in an arbitration clause in a contract is a separate (and autonomous) agreement from the rest of the contract. This is the doctrine of the "separability" or "autonomy" of the arbitration clause. Accordingly, the termination or avoidance (for example, following a fraudulent misrepresentation) of a contract which was initially valid will not affect the validity of the arbitration agreement. The doctrine also recognises in this way the wish of the parties to have disputes arising out of their contract settled by arbitration, even if that contract is no longer in existence. The separability of the arbitration clause is confirmed in the same articles which deal with the power to decide on jurisdiction (see above).

One difficulty remains, and that is when the initial validity of the underlying contract is in question. If the parties failed to conclude a contract at all, that could affect the validity not only of the contract itself, but also of the arbitration agreement. Where the parties have failed to do what is necessary to conclude a contract, it is difficult, though not impossible (note, in this respect, Article 6(4) of the ICC Arbitration Rules) to see why they might have intended that an arbitration agreement should come into existence. In such a case, the tribunal is unlikely to have any jurisdiction. (This situation should be distinguished from one where the existence of the arbitration agreement itself is in question. Article 7 of the UNCITRAL Model Law sets out the requirements for a valid arbitration agreement.)

The options available to a party which challenges the entire jurisdiction of a tribunal are similar to those available where the challenge is only partial. However, because the challenge is to the entire jurisdiction of the tribunal, that party may decide to ignore the arbitration proceedings altogether. If the tribunal makes an award against the challenging party, that party may then apply to the state courts to have the award set aside or defend recognition or enforcement proceedings brought in a foreign state, on the basis that the tribunal lacked jurisdiction.

Many respondents are unwilling to commit themselves to such a "hands-off" course, particularly as it involves the risk that if the state court finds against them on the issue of jurisdiction, they will not have been heard on any of the issues going to the merits of the dispute. The safer, and more usual, course is for the party to raise the issue of jurisdiction with the tribunal (if the tribunal has power to deal with it) or to continue to participate in the arbitration under protest as to jurisdiction (if the tribunal does not have such power).

If the tribunal rules that it does have jurisdiction, the respondent may be able to apply immediately to the state courts at the seat of the arbitration for that decision to be set aside (see page 78 above). On a more aggressive note, the challenging party may decide to dispose of the dispute altogether by commencing legal proceedings challenging the substance of the dispute between the parties and leaving it to the claimant in the arbitration to try and halt the proceedings on the basis that there is a valid arbitration agreement.

Finally, recognition or enforcement of the award may be resisted in a foreign state, save that in this case it will be Article V(1)(a), and not Article V(1)(c), of the New York Convention that will be relevant (see option (d) under the heading "Partial challenge" above).

THE POWERS OF THE TRIBUNAL

Source and purpose

As indicated at the beginning of this chapter, the primary source for the powers of the tribunal is the arbitration agreement (including any arbitration rules incorporated by reference into that agreement). After that, reference should be made to the law applicable to the arbitration agreement and finally the law applicable to the arbitration proceedings (i.e. at the seat).

The powers given to a tribunal should be those which are regarded as necessary to ensure the efficient conduct of the arbitration through to the making of an award. A tribunal is usually not obliged to exercise its powers. Thus, for example, if it has the power to appoint experts, it is not under an obligation to do so. This is to be contrasted with the position on jurisdiction. A tribunal which has jurisdiction to deal with a dispute must deal with that dispute, if it is submitted to it. It should be noted that a tribunal cannot usually delegate its powers to a third party.

The rules of most arbitration institutions, as well as the UNCITRAL Arbitration Rules, give the tribunal wide powers and discretion for the conduct of the arbitration, such as the power to decide all procedural and evidential matters. As the tribunal becomes more involved in the arbitration and as it comes to understand the issues involved and the nature of the evidence which may be required to dispose of them, it is likely to become increasingly assertive as to the manner in which it considers that the proceedings should be conducted. Nevertheless, a tribunal would be unwise to attempt to impose a direction on the parties which runs contrary to the express wishes of both of them: awards not made in accordance with the procedure agreed on by the parties may be set aside, or will not be capable of recognition or enforcement. In such a case, the tribunal should attempt to persuade the parties so that at least one of them comes to agree with the tribunal's approach and ultimately agrees to the direction.

The parties may, in the light of the nature of any anticipated dispute between them, decide to give the tribunal special powers. For example, the parties to an arbitration agreement contained in a contract for a substantial construction project may give the tribunal power to call on the parties to give it access to the site, so that it can inspect the building which is the subject of dispute.

An important point is that the powers of the tribunal may be limited. Parties cannot confer on a tribunal powers beyond those permitted by the law applicable to the arbitration agreement or to the arbitration proceedings. This is especially important for those who are not parties to the arbitration. Thus the arbitral tribunal may not (in most states) compel the attendance of third parties as witnesses at hearings or require them to produce documents for the tribunal (even if the parties' agreement purports to give it power to do so). (An exception to this is in the USA, where arbitral tribunals have such power by law.) This highlights the importance of the supporting role of the courts at the seat of the arbitration. Only the courts have the power to compel a witness to attend before a tribunal or to order the preservation of property or evidence in the hands of a third party, and even then only if permitted to do so by their own law.

Compliance with the tribunal's directions

The tribunal's powers are of little worth unless the tribunal is able to secure compliance with its directions or, failing that, continue with the proceedings in the absence of compliance. The parties to most arbitrations do comply with the tribunal's directions. Occasionally the time within which a pleading must be served is overrun. There is little that a tribunal can, or will, do about that (save for expressing its displeasure). From time to time, however, and with a view to causing maximum disruption to the proceedings, a party flagrantly refuses to comply with a direction.

The problem may be compounded where the tribunal has given directions as to the dates for service of the statement of defence as well as the commencement of the hearing. If, for no good reason, the respondent serves its statement of defence very late, and only days before the commencement of the hearing, the tribunal could find itself in a quandary. If it allows the defence to be included in the proceedings, the hearing may have to be postponed in order to allow the claimant sufficient time to deal with the allegations contained in the defence. If it disallows the defence, it runs the risk of an application to set aside the award on the basis that the tribunal has failed to give the respondent a full opportunity to present its case.

These problems are circumvented in properly drafted arbitration rules, in that they will specifically permit the tribunal to continue with the proceedings in the absence of the defence (see, for example, Article 28 of the UNCITRAL Arbitration Rules). In the absence of such rules, the law applicable to the arbitration proceedings may provide a similar solution (see, for example, section 41 of the English Arbitration Act 1996 and Article 25 of the UNCITRAL Model Law). In practice, these powers are rarely exercised because tribunals and courts are very reluctant to shut out a defence.

Whilst the tribunal's power to secure compliance with its directions is limited, it can penalise a party when awarding costs at the end of the proceedings (or at an interim stage, if the tribunal is empowered to do so). Tribunals often take into account the conduct of the parties during the proceedings when making decisions on costs. A party who, for example, deliberately employs delaying tactics or causes wasted costs by calling unnecessary evidence may be penalised by a tribunal on costs.

THE TRIBUNAL'S OBLIGATIONS

Source and nature

The arbitration agreement, the law applicable to the arbitration agreement and the law applicable to the arbitration proceedings will be relevant when identifying the tribunal's obligations. They should be considered in that order.

There are two kinds of obligation imposed by the arbitration agreement:

(a) Those expressly set out by the parties in their agreement; and
(b) Those referred to indirectly (i.e. in arbitration rules incorporated into the arbitration agreement).

Examples of the former are the obligation to act as amiable compositeurs (see page 16 above), if required to do so by the parties, or to conduct the arbitration proceedings in the language agreed upon by the parties. An example of the latter is the obligation of a tribunal, in an arbitration conducted under the UNCITRAL Arbitration Rules, to give the parties adequate advance notice of the date of an oral hearing (Article 25(1)).

Obligations may also be imposed by law. Many countries have adopted the UNCITRAL Model Law as the basis for their national law and where this is the case, the law will set out certain express obligations, including:

(a) to act without undue delay (Article 14(1));
(b) to treat the parties with equality and to give each of them a full opportunity to present its case (or, as it is sometimes expressed, to act impartially) (Article 18);
(c) to take into account applicable trade usages (Article 28(4)); and
(d) to sign the award (Article 31(1)).

In states that have not adopted the UNCITRAL Model Law, the tribunal's obligations may be more difficult to establish.

The principle of equality requires some elaboration. The whole purpose of arbitration would be defeated if the parties were not to be treated with equality by the arbitral tribunal, or if either were to be deprived of a full opportunity to present its case.

If the parties are to be treated with equality, the members of the arbitral tribunal must be independent and impartial. If any one of them is not, the laws of most states, and the rules of arbitration institutions, permit the removal of that arbitrator. To be independent, an arbitrator should not have any financial interest in the outcome of the arbitration, nor have any professional connection with any of the parties. Any lack of independence should be notified immediately to the parties who, after assessing it, can decide whether the arbitrator may continue with the reference or should be removed.

The International Bar Association (IBA) published in 2004 *Guidelines on Conflicts of Interest in International Arbitration*. The aim of the guidelines is to encourage consistency in the standards applied by arbitrators and practitioners in deciding whether there is a conflict of interest and whether certain situations need to be disclosed. The guidelines comprise general standards on impartiality, independence and disclosure and then set out three lists: the red list (clear cases of conflict of interest), the orange list (situations which may present a conflict of interest and should be disclosed) and the green list (situations which do not merit disclosure). The guidelines are published at *www.ibanet.org/pdf/ InternationalArbitrationGuidelines.pdf*.

An arbitrator should also refrain from communicating with one only of the parties (e.g. oral communications made in the absence of the other party or written communications where a copy of the document is not sent to the other party at the same time). An arbitrator is "partial" if he or she manifests a prejudice against one of the parties, or against a particular outcome to a dispute.

In this respect, two situations often present difficulty to parties to an arbitration. The first situation is the position of the party-appointed arbitrator on an arbitral tribunal of three members. Arbitrators are often nominated by a party because they are thought to have some sympathy with the party or its cause (in this sense it is sometimes said that an arbitrator does not have to be "neutral" – i.e. of different nationality and economic and political background). That, of itself, is only to be expected and is unobjectionable, so long as the arbitrator does not permit any feelings of empathy to determine the manner in which functions as arbitrator are exercised.

The second situation concerns the sole arbitrator or chairman of a tribunal who is of the same nationality as one of the parties. Again, there is nothing inherently wrong with this, though the rules of a number of the arbitration institutions do, as a precautionary measure, forbid it, unless the parties agree otherwise.

There is also the right of a party to a full opportunity to present its case. It is impossible to provide an objective definition of this right, as much will depend on the circumstances existing at the relevant time. That said, the existence of the right does not require an arbitral tribunal to permit a party to make an oral presentation for whatever length of time that party may think appropriate. The arbitral tribunal has the power, indeed the obligation, to control the proceedings and to ensure that the dispute is disposed of expeditiously. In doing so, however, it must ensure that the parties are given the same opportunities to present their cases and that they are given a chance to address all the real issues in the dispute.

The arbitral tribunal is under a general duty to keep the subject-matter of the arbitration confidential unless the parties consent to its disclosure. This duty of confidentiality is contained in some laws and rules (see, for example, Article 30(2) of the LCIA Arbitration Rules). This obligation on the arbitral tribunal should be distinguished from the duty of confidentiality binding the parties (see page 37 above).

Absent from the list of obligations set out above is an "obligation to act with care". This does not mean that arbitrators in an arbitration taking place in a state which has adopted the UNCITRAL Model Law are not under an obligation to act with care. Such an obligation may be found elsewhere in the relevant country's law, for example in its law of contract or tort or delict.

The consequences of, and remedies for, breach of obligation

The important and practical question is: "What happens if a tribunal fails to honour its obligations and what can be done about that failure?" The simplest way of considering this is to do so by reference to the principal stages in an international arbitration.

(a) *During the course of the arbitration proceedings*: Important obligations at this stage are the obligations to act impartially and without undue delay and to provide adequate notice of hearings. If dealt with early enough, certain defaults on the part of an arbitrator can be remedied. An arbitrator who has been slow in dealing with communications from the parties or in the preparation of an interim award may well respond positively to a polite but firm request that he answer the communications. Where insufficient notice of a hearing has been given, the arbitrator may be asked to reconsider the date and to fix a more convenient one. Apparently partial behaviour may be put right by persuading the arbitrator to hear, for example, the evidence that would otherwise have been excluded.

In brief, an attempt at persuasion is usually the best first step, because it will not have the effect of disrupting, and causing further delay to, the arbitration proceedings. There may, however, be occasions when the manifestation of partiality is so gross, or delay is so great (notwithstanding pleas for urgency), that more formal steps must be taken to rectify matters. Partiality and undue delay are both grounds for the removal of an arbitrator. The procedure for, and the consequences of, removal are set out at pages 72–74 above.

Where one of a number of arbitrators refuses to sign the award, the signatures of the majority are usually sufficient (see, for example, Article 31(1) of the UNCITRAL Model Law, and Article 26(4) of the LCIA Arbitration Rules).

(b) *After the award has been made*: Once the award has been made, the misdemeanours of an arbitrator have to be considered in the light of their possible effect on the validity of the award. Delay, inconvenient though it may have been, is unlikely to affect validity unless the tribunal has failed to make its award within the period of time which may have been required of it by the arbitration agreement or the rules or the law applicable to the arbitration. However, where an arbitrator has been partial in the conduct of the arbitration, this will be a ground for the setting aside of the award. Another ground for setting aside an award is the failure of the tribunal to conduct the arbitration in accordance with the procedure agreed upon by the parties.

The matters relevant in the context of setting aside an award are dealt with at pages 128–130 below.

(c) *On an application for the recognition or enforcement of the award in a foreign country*: Grounds for resisting an application for the recognition or enforcement of an award under the New York Convention include:
   (i) the inability of a party to present its case (Article V(1)(b));
   (ii) the departure by the tribunal from the procedure agreed upon by the parties (Article V(1)(d)); and
   (iii) the contravention of the public policy of the country in which recognition or enforcement is sought (Article V(2)(b)), as where it is discovered that an arbitrator has accepted a bribe to make the award in a particular manner.

The relevant procedure is dealt with at pages 130–133 below.

Having dealt with the effects of breaches by an arbitrator on the conduct of the proceedings, the award and any attempt to have the award recognised or enforced, one can then consider their effect on the parties. Unnecessary delay by an arbitrator will probably cause additional loss to a successful claimant because it has been deprived of its money for longer and the interest included in the award is unlikely to compensate fully for the claimant's loss. A deserving claimant may be deprived of its entitlement as a result of the carelessness of the arbitrator in conducting the proceedings and preparing the award or, worse still, as a result of the arbitrator taking a bribe from the other party.

Establishing liability for unreasonable delay on the part of an arbitrator is not common. The rules of the principal arbitration institutions do not provide for it, but there is such provision in some national laws. Whilst it does not render an arbitrator liable for delay, sections 24(1) and (4) of the English Arbitration Act 1996 provide that an arbitrator removed for failing to use "all reasonable dispatch" may not be entitled to any remuneration.

Fixing an arbitrator with liability for an act or omission (including carelessness or bribe-taking) in the course of the arbitration is complicated by policy considerations. The laws of many states give an arbitrator immunity from proceedings in respect of his conduct during the arbitration, so that the right people should not be discouraged from taking up appointments as arbitrators, and to keep to a minimum proceedings which may be ancillary to an arbitration. Where it does exist, the immunity must be checked carefully. It may not be as extensive as it appears at first sight. Furthermore, it cannot reasonably be argued that the policy consideration underlying the immunity requires that protection should be given to an arbitrator who has acted not just carelessly, but in bad faith.

CHAPTER 7

THE PROCEEDINGS

INTRODUCTION

Once the arbitration has been commenced and the tribunal has been appointed, the proceedings may begin. During the course of the proceedings:

(a) the issues between the parties must be established;

(b) the relevant evidence must be made available to the tribunal;

(c) the parties must be given the opportunity to make submissions on the issues and the evidence; and

(d) the tribunal must be given the opportunity to clarify with the parties their arguments on the issues and the evidence.

It is one of the benefits of arbitration, as opposed to litigation, that the parties can usually choose and adapt the procedure which is to be used in the course of the arbitration. Thus, they can exclude some of the more cumbersome procedures which may be found in state court proceedings.

The ability of the parties to choose the procedure for an arbitration and tailor it to their own requirements limits the scope for generalisation about procedural matters. However, this chapter will examine the steps that are common to many arbitrations (e.g. a preliminary meeting, terms of reference, written submissions, evidence and the hearing itself) and some of the issues which need to be considered along the way.

Objectives of the proceedings

It is important to remember the principal objectives of the proceedings. These are:

(a) to establish the facts to be able to determine the rights and obligations of the parties; and

(b) to reach an award which is enforceable.

Establishing the facts of a case can be difficult and expensive. A balance has to be struck between taking too long and spending too much in an attempt to establish every fact, and not doing enough to establish sufficient facts to achieve an award which reflects the case that has been brought.

Superimposed on this dilemma is the division between those who think that the best way to establish the facts is to let the parties test each other's evidence, and those who think that the facts will best emerge if a neutral third party (i.e. the judge or arbitrator) has the obligation to investigate them. Traditionally, civil law systems require the judge or arbitrator to establish the facts, whereas common law systems have put that burden principally on the parties themselves. A traditional criticism levelled at civil law systems is that, since the judge or arbitrator (or court-appointed expert – see page 103 below) has no personal interest in the proceedings, the tribunal is only as diligent in investigating the facts as it wants to be. Furthermore, it is also said that civil law judges and arbitrators tend to take at face value the evidence of a court-appointed expert, without testing its accuracy or completeness. On the other hand, parties criticise common law systems for resulting in far greater expenditure in terms of legal and expert costs and lengthier proceedings.

As for ensuring that an award is enforceable, care must always be taken to ensure that the proceedings are conducted in a manner which does not jeopardise that objective. In particular, they should be conducted in accordance with the fundamental principle that the parties are to be treated equally and fairly.

Subject to what is said below, the tribunal must also conduct the proceedings in accordance with the procedure agreed by the parties (the principle of party autonomy, which has already been referred to at page 9 above). If it does not, there is a risk that one of the parties will seek to have the award set aside or resist enforcement of it (Article V(1)(d) of the New York Convention).

There are two important limitations on the principle of party autonomy. The first relates to what must or must not be done in the proceedings. The second relates to control of the proceedings and the extent to which the arbitral tribunal can impose its wishes on the parties.

As to the first limitation, the procedure agreed upon by the parties will always be subject to the mandatory requirements of the law which is applicable to the arbitration proceedings (i.e. the law of the seat of the arbitration). As to the second, by agreeing to arbitrate in accordance with the rules of an arbitral institution (which usually include rules relating to the conduct of proceedings), the parties have agreed that the proceedings shall be conducted in accordance with the procedure established by the institution. Some institutions, such as the LCIA, make it clear that the parties can depart from the rules and establish their own procedure for the arbitration (see Article 14(1) of the LCIA Arbitration Rules). The rules of some other institutions do permit the parties a good deal of scope in what they may agree upon by way of procedure, but specifically leave control in the hands of the tribunal (see Articles 1(1) and 16(1) of the AAA/ICDR's International Arbitration Rules). CIETAC allows parties to agree to depart from its rules, but only where the Arbitration Commission consents to such agreement (see Article 7 of the CIETAC Arbitration Rules).

Control of the proceedings can sometimes be a difficult and sensitive issue, involving a conflict between:

(a) the wishes of the parties as to how they want their arbitration to be conducted, and
(b) what may be necessary for the efficient resolution of the dispute.

As the proceedings progress and as the arbitral tribunal obtains a clearer view of which issues are important and which peripheral (and of the evidence which may be required in order to try them), the tribunal may become more assertive about how the proceedings should be conducted. However, a tribunal should be cautious about imposing a procedural direction on the parties if the parties have not agreed that a different procedure is appropriate. In some circumstances, such a decision could render the award unenforceable. If the parties have not agreed the appropriate procedure, the tribunal must give directions.

THE PRELIMINARY MEETING

As with most commercial activities, arbitration proceedings will be conducted more effectively and efficiently if adequate plans have been made for their conduct. Chapter 3 contains a discussion of some of the planning which can take place at the time that the arbitration agreement is being prepared. However, many arbitration agreements are not carefully thought out and, even when they are, circumstances may have changed by the time a dispute arises. It is therefore common for a tribunal to hold, at an early stage in the proceedings, a preliminary meeting (or preliminary conference, as it is called in some states) to discuss and, if possible, agree the procedure and timetable for the arbitration. In ICC proceedings such a meeting is likely to be used to finalise and sign the Terms of Reference. In large and complex arbitrations there may be a second or third preliminary meeting convened, as time goes on, to take account of changing circumstances or, where insufficient information has been made available to the tribunal at the time of its appointment, to deal with matters arising later on in the arbitration as and when that information becomes available.

Form

The parties and the tribunal should, and usually do, meet face to face (although in very simple cases the matters to be covered can be dealt with entirely by correspondence or by telephone). The form and length of the preliminary meeting depend on:

(a) Whether or not the parties come from the same legal background. Parties from similar backgrounds may agree more readily on the procedure to be followed than parties from divergent backgrounds.

(b) Whether the case is procedurally complex. This will depend, amongst other things, upon the number of parties, the number of factual issues to be dealt with, the extent to which expert evidence is required (and the corresponding number of expert witnesses), the volume of documentation which has to be managed and any linguistic problems which have to be overcome.

(c) The attitude of the parties and their advisors. If one (or both) is unreasonable, or is trying to gain an advantage by manipulating the arbitration procedure, the conduct of the meeting can become difficult.

Timing

A preliminary meeting cannot be held until the arbitral tribunal has been appointed and has been sent sufficient information to enable it to identify the principal issues between the parties. Furthermore, in the case of some institutional arbitrations (such as arbitrations conducted under the ICC's Arbitration Rules) there may be administrative preliminaries which have to be completed (e.g. the administrative fees must have been paid to the ICC and the impartiality of the arbitrator(s) checked, so that the "file" containing the request, the response and other correspondence, can be sent to the tribunal) before the tribunal can convene the preliminary meeting.

Preparation

Adequate preparation for the preliminary meeting must be undertaken by both the arbitrators and the parties (and their advisers). This preparatory work consists of thinking through the arrangements for the conduct of the preliminary meeting itself (e.g. the time and venue for the meeting and whether there are any arrangements which may have to be made to assist the arbitrators in getting to the venue), as well as the agenda items to be dealt with at the meeting. The parties should not prepare in isolation. An arbitration will run much more smoothly if the parties are able to discuss the procedure and agree upon its important elements (and, where they disagree, to notify the arbitral tribunal beforehand of the disagreement so that the arbitrators may come to the meeting prepared to deal with it).

Items for the agenda

There are no specific rules as to what has to be discussed at a preliminary meeting. The purpose of the meeting is to plan for the expeditious and efficient conduct of the arbitration. Accordingly, all matters relevant to that should be considered. UNCITRAL has produced useful guidelines entitled *Notes on Organising Arbitral Proceedings*. These guidelines (which are not binding on parties and which can be a useful basis even in those arbitrations which are not conducted in accordance with the UNCITRAL Arbitration Rules) can be used as a checklist of matters which may (not must) be considered at a preliminary meeting. UNCITRAL stresses, in notes accompanying the guidelines, that the guidelines do not form "comprehensive guidance" on the matters to be dealt with at a preliminary meeting. The agenda items include (in the order they are set out in the guidelines):

(a) *Arbitration rules*: Where the arbitration is non-institutional and no agreed rules have been incorporated into the arbitration agreement, the parties may wish to agree on the adoption of a set of rules (e.g. the UNCITRAL Arbitration Rules).

(b) *Language*: Even if agreement has been reached on the language in which the proceedings are to be conducted, it may also be necessary for directions to be given as to the translation of documents which may be produced during the course of the proceedings. If there is to be oral testimony, the meeting should consider how best this is to be translated and which party is to bear the costs of translation.

(c) *Seat of the arbitration*: If the seat of the arbitration has not already been agreed upon, or confirmed by the institution by which the arbitration is being administered, it is up to the tribunal to determine the place of arbitration at the preliminary meeting (for the importance of this, see page 27 above). A proviso which is frequently added is that the tribunal is free to meet and to hold hearings in such other places as it considers convenient. This proviso will not alter the law which is applicable to the proceedings, but it will make the administration of the arbitration easier and prevent any subsequent challenges to an award made on the basis that the tribunal has failed to comply with the procedure established for the arbitration.

(d) *Costs*: In the case of many institutional arbitrations (such as those conducted under the ICC's Arbitration Rules), the institution itself will determine the administrative fees to be charged, the security against the costs of the arbitration to be provided by the parties, and, ultimately, the arbitrators' fees. Where the arbitration is non-institutional, it is the members of the tribunal itself who have to agree the level of their fees (see page 70 above) and determine how much they will require from the parties as an advance against their fees, when that advance should be paid, how it should be dealt with until paid out to the arbitrators and what happens if an increase is required during the course of the proceedings.

(e) *Communications*: A system will have to be put in place for the transmission of documents between the tribunal and the parties (and, where appropriate, the arbitration institution). The most effective system is for the parties to exchange documents between themselves, sending a copy of formal submission to each member of the tribunal. It must also be established that any communication between a party and a member of the tribunal has to be copied to the other party. In most arbitrations, ordinary correspondence between the parties or their advisers should not be copied to the tribunal. Communication by electronic mail and fax is very common, particularly where the hard copy will follow. However, thought should be given in such circumstances as to which mode of communication will be the controlling one for the purpose of time limits. Where communication or exchange will only be in electronic form, it may be vital to agree on technical matters such as, for example, electronic file formats and media to be used. (See further page 106 below on the use of information technology in arbitration.)

(f) *Timing of written submissions*: As indicated above, one of the principal purposes of the preliminary meeting is to set a timetable for the proceedings. An essential element in this process is the setting of deadlines by which written submissions have to be prepared. This requires a balance to be struck between the possible (i.e. what the parties can reasonably be expected to do) and the ideal (i.e. ensuring that the proceedings are kept moving quickly).

(g) *The form of the written submissions*: In an institutional arbitration, the rules of the institution may provide some guidance as to the form of the submissions. In the case of non-institutional arbitrations, there is seldom agreement beforehand on the form of the submissions, although where the arbitration is conducted under the UNCITRAL Arbitration Rules, Articles 18 and 19 of those rules do establish requirements as to form and they may be used as a model. (See also pages 97–99 below.)

(h) *The evidence*: The UNCITRAL guidelines highlight the importance of making adequate provision for the manner in which the evidence is to be dealt with, particularly where the parties come from different legal backgrounds. This is clearly important in relation to disclosure of documents (i.e. the practice in some common law legal systems that, subject to the exception of those documents which are protected by legal privilege, parties produce for inspection by each other all documents which are relevant to the issues between them, and which are in their possession or control). However, it is also important in the context of dealing with witness statements and expert evidence (see pages 102–104 below).

(i) *Preliminary issues*: The preliminary meeting is a suitable occasion for discussing whether there are any issues which should be dealt with at a preliminary hearing and, if so, how they are to be dealt with. Such issues may be procedural (going, for example, to the jurisdiction of the tribunal) or substantive (for example, a legal point which, if decided one way, may dispense with the need for detailed submissions and evidence at a later stage in the arbitration proceedings).

(j) *Hearings*: Most arbitration proceedings include one or more hearings. Subject to agreement between them to the contrary, it is generally accepted that parties have a right to a hearing. Because parties and/or arbitrators are probably going to have to come to the hearings from different states, it is important that arrangements for hearings are made sufficiently far in advance so that those concerned can make the necessary bookings for a set of rooms for the hearing and for travel. Other matters which may be dealt with include the following.

 (i) Whether there should be any limit on the amount of time each of the parties has for oral arguments and questioning witnesses.

 (ii) The presentation of witness evidence. Witness statements or statements of evidence are used extensively to set out the primary evidence from a witness and are usually exchanged well before the hearing.

(iii) The number of witnesses. A tribunal may limit the number of witnesses a party can utilise, either in total or on a particular issue(s) in the dispute. This is particularly the case with expert or technical evidence where a limit of one expert witness on a topic may be directed.

(iv) The order in which the parties will present their arguments and evidence.

 (v) The length of the hearing(s).

(vi) Whether arrangements have to be made for the preparation of an electronic or other transcript of the hearings.

(vii) Emergency matters. In the event that one party seeks an urgent hearing, how practically and procedurally that is to be achieved.

After the preliminary meeting

Once the preliminary meeting has been concluded the tribunal will issue, and send to the parties, directions for the conduct of the arbitration. Where the parties have so agreed, these directions may be signed and sent out by the chairman (if any) alone of the arbitral tribunal, thus removing a cause of delay whilst the directions are circulated to the other members of the tribunal for signature.

TERMS OF REFERENCE

Many arbitrations, particularly those which are non-institutional and which are conducted in common law countries, are conducted without resort to terms of reference. However, terms of reference are required by Article 18 of the ICC Arbitration Rules in ICC arbitrations and they are also often used in international arbitrations not governed by the ICC Arbitration Rules.

The role of terms of reference

The present role of terms of reference developed from the requirement (now largely replaced) of certain legal systems that the parties had to sign a "submission agreement" after the dispute had arisen, in order for the arbitration to be valid. The purpose of the submission agreement was to evidence their clear agreement:

(a) to forgo the right to have the dispute dealt with in the state courts; and
(b) to submit their dispute to arbitration.

As already indicated, the ICC has maintained a role for terms of reference and other tribunals sometimes adopt their use because their preparation carries with it certain advantages. These may include:

(a) The definition of the issues in the case. This is helpful in focusing the minds of the parties, and of the tribunal, on what the dispute between the parties is really about.
(b) The definition and the clarification of the extent of the arbitrator's jurisdiction. This can make more difficult a subsequent challenge to an award on the ground, for example, that the tribunal exceeded its authority.

The preparation of the terms of reference will usually take place once the parties have exchanged their initial submissions (thus permitting the identification of the issues in the arbitration) but before submission of the parties' respective statement of case. Sometimes parts of the terms of reference will overlap with directions given at a preliminary meeting.

Contents

The contents of the terms of reference will depend upon what the parties have agreed they should contain. An illustration of the kind of matters to be covered is provided by Article 18(1) of the ICC Arbitration Rules, which provides that the terms of reference in an ICC arbitration must include the following matters.

(a) The full names and descriptions of the parties and the addresses of the parties to which notifications or communications arising in the course of the arbitration may validly be made.
(b) A summary of the parties' respective claims and the relief sought. This may, unless the tribunal thinks it inappropriate, set out a list of the issues to be determined. It may be difficult, in a large and complicated case, to summarise all of the parties' respective contentions as to the facts and the law. It will often only be possible to set out a brief summary of the principal arguments, whilst repeating the entirety of the formal request for relief (i.e. the requests made by each party for specific orders, which are contained at the end of their submissions).
(c) The names, description and addresses of the arbitrators.
(d) The place of arbitration (i.e. the seat of the arbitration).
(e) Particulars of the applicable procedural rules and, if such is the case, reference to the power conferred upon the arbitrator to act as amiable compositeur (see page 16 above).

Article 18(4) makes provision for the establishment, in a separate document, of a provisional timetable for the conduct of the arbitration.

Parties to an ICC arbitration should note that Article 19 of the ICC Arbitration Rules does not allow new claims to be made that fall outside the limits of the terms of reference, unless authorised by the tribunal.

Drafting

Article 18 of the ICC Arbitration Rules provides that the tribunal shall draw up the terms of reference on the basis of documents, or in the presence of the parties, and in light of their most recent submissions. In international arbitrations where the ICC Arbitration Rules do not apply, it will often be the parties who are responsible for the drafting of the terms of reference. Where the tribunal has a civil law background it is more likely that the tribunal may draft the terms of reference. In any event, the terms of reference will be signed by the tribunal and the parties.

The unco-operative party

Occasionally a party (particularly one which contests the jurisdiction of the tribunal) may refuse to co-operate in the preparation of terms of reference or to sign them. Where this happens, it is important to distinguish between those cases where the terms of reference are a necessary part of the arbitration procedure (as, for example, in cases administered by the ICC) and those where they are not necessary, but are merely considered desirable. In the latter case, the lack of co-operation will amount to little more than a procedural irritant and a lost opportunity to establish clearly the basis upon which the arbitration is to be conducted. In the case of the former, the rules should (as Article 18(3) of the ICC Arbitration Rules does) provide a mechanism for the continuation of the arbitration notwithstanding the failure to co-operate.

THE WRITTEN SUBMISSIONS

Almost every arbitration will involve the parties in an exchange of written submissions. Properly prepared submissions are the most efficient means of ensuring that the arbitral tribunal and the opposing parties are aware at an early stage of what the case is about. The submissions should describe the circumstances giving rise to the dispute, set out the respective claims, identify the issues and, in those cases in which it is required (as under the rules of some institutions), identify the evidence relied on. In this respect they are like pleadings and will provide the legal and factual framework on which the hearings will be based. Submissions may also be prepared to cover arguments on specific legal issues.

The form of written submissions will depend on two principal factors:

(a) the requirements of any agreement between the parties, or applicable institutional rules, as to the form and content of submissions; and

(b) any directions which may have been given by the tribunal.

It may also be influenced by the legal background of the person preparing the submissions, e.g. whether it is a common law or civil law system, and by the legal background of the member(s) of the tribunal.

Institutional requirements

It is not possible to list the requirements laid down by each institution for written submissions. Some institutions, such as the ICC, have very little in their rules with regard to the preparation of submissions. Others, such as the LCIA and ICSID, have a good deal more. In large and complex arbitrations conducted under the ICC Arbitration Rules an outline only of the case will be provided in the request for arbitration, though the claimant may well be required, usually after the first preliminary meeting, to prepare a more detailed statement of case. Where the arbitration is conducted under the LCIA Arbitration Rules, the claimant is merely required, in the request for arbitration, to provide a brief statement describing the nature and circumstances of the dispute, and specifying the relief claimed. However, within 30 days of receipt of notification of the appointment of the tribunal, the claimant must submit its statement of case setting out in sufficient detail the facts and any contentions of law on which it relies, as well as the relief claimed. After receipt of the statement of case the respondent must, within a specified period of time, serve a statement of defence, or answer, which should be prepared in a form similar to that required for the statement of case. That statement of defence should also include, where appropriate, any counterclaim. It is a common requirement that the parties should serve, with their statements, copies of the documents upon which they intend to rely.

Time limits

The timetable for the service of written submissions will usually be contained in:

(a) any rules (including those of an arbitration institution) which the parties have agreed should govern the arbitration procedure (in the case of non-institutional arbitration, the parties may have set out the timetable in their arbitration agreement); and

(b) directions made by the tribunal.

Time limits may, in most cases, be extended by agreement between the parties or, failing agreement, by direction from the tribunal. Where a party has failed to prepare its submission in time and has not obtained an extension of time, the tribunal may, upon giving reasonable notice to the party, proceed with the arbitration and ignore the contents of a submission which is subsequently served. Ideally, an attempt should be made at the outset to set realistic time limits for the preparation and service of submissions. If too tight a timetable is established, with a hearing fixed to follow closely behind submissions, failure to adhere to the timetable might jeopardise the date for the hearing itself. If that date has to be vacated, there may be considerable delay whilst an attempt is made to find a mutually convenient date for a re-fixed hearing.

EVIDENCE

As with other questions of procedure, the parties are generally free to agree on how evidence is to be dealt with (subject to any mandatory rules of the law applicable to the arbitration proceedings). However, the approach to evidence differs enormously around the world. That would not necessarily matter a great deal if evidence were merely an incidental matter in arbitration proceedings, but questions of evidence lie at the heart of most of them. This, coupled with the very different approaches to evidence, makes dealing with evidence in international arbitration a difficult subject. This is all the more so when the parties' legal advisers try to insist on adhering to procedures relating to evidence which are applicable to court proceedings in their home countries.

Because of these difficulties, in 1983 a committee of the International Bar Association drew up rules governing the presentation and reception of evidence in international commercial arbitration in an attempt to establish procedures which would be acceptable to parties, no matter what their legal background, and which would lead to more efficiently conducted arbitrations. Parties may agree to apply the rules, in whole or in part, to their proceedings. The rules were revised and updated in June 1999 as the IBA Rules on the Taking of Evidence in International Commercial Arbitration (commonly referred to as the "IBA Rules of Evidence"). Relevant parts of these rules are discussed below.

Technical rules of evidence

Technical rules of evidence are those provisions contained in the law applicable to the arbitration proceedings which relate to matters such as the admissibility of items of evidence (for example, whether a second-hand, or "hearsay", account of an event may be used in the arbitration proceedings as evidence of a party's contentions with regard to the event) or whether a party may give evidence in support of its own case. The general position internationally is that an arbitrator may ignore particular technical rules of evidence which have their origin and application in the proceedings of state courts. This is borne out in the following:

(a) State arbitration laws – see, for example, sections 34(1) and 34(2)(f) of the English Arbitration Act 1996, Article 1039(5) of the Netherlands Arbitration Act 1986, Article 1460 of the French Code of Civil Procedure and Article 19(2) of the UNCITRAL Model Law.

(b) Institutional rules – see Article 20(6) of the AAA/ICDR's International Arbitration Rules and Article 15(1) of the ICC Arbitration Rules.

(c) Non-institutional rules – see Article 25(6) of the UNCITRAL Arbitration Rules.

Whilst of decreasing importance, the significance of technical rules of evidence is that failure to apply them, where they do apply, may provide a ground for resisting an application for enforcement of an award under the New York Convention (see Article V(1)(d), which applies where the arbitral procedure was not in accordance with the arbitration law of the seat of the arbitration). However, if the party resisting enforcement has not raised an objection to the failure to apply the technical rules within a reasonable period of time, that objection may be treated as waived under some arbitration rules (see, for example, Article 30 of the UNCITRAL Arbitration Rules). Furthermore, the existence of technical rules of evidence in the procedural laws of a state, applicable to its courts, does not of itself require that such rules be applied to international arbitration conducted in that state. The true question is what, if any, requirements as to evidence (and other such technical points of procedure) are made by the arbitration law of that state.

Burden of proof

Each party has the burden of proving the facts relied on to support its claim or defence. The standard of proof (i.e. the degree or extent to which a party must establish a fact to the satisfaction of the tribunal) has no clear definition in international commercial arbitration. It is, however, generally accepted that the test is that the tribunal should be satisfied that the fact alleged is "more likely than not" or that the fact is "on the balance of probability" as alleged.

It is an important function of the tribunal to determine the weight (or importance) to attach to the evidence before it. Arbitrators commonly give more weight to evidence contained in contemporaneous documents (i.e. those documents created in the course of the negotiation or performance of a contract) than to the oral evidence of a witness given at the hearing.

Documents

There are two broad categories of documents:

(a) those which the parties produce voluntarily to each other, and to the tribunal, in support of the allegations made by them; and

(b) those which they produce to the other party under compulsion.

Documents which are produced voluntarily are seldom the source of procedural difficulty, unless it is alleged that they have been forged or falsified in some way. The tribunal will, nonetheless, have to interpret them and decide how much weight is to be attached to them as evidence.

The production of documents by compulsion is more complex, particularly if the parties have not reached agreement on the extent to which production can be compelled. The problems are exacerbated if the parties come from different legal backgrounds and have, as a result, different approaches to dealing with documents in proceedings.

In common law countries, parties to state court proceedings are commonly required to make disclosure of documents (see page 94 above). A tribunal may draw adverse inferences from a failure to produce documents which are known to exist or to have existed. Where an arbitration relates to a substantial contract performed over several years, a requirement for discovery of all relevant documents can have the consequence that the parties are burdened with a huge paper exercise. Thus, even though this increases the likelihood that all relevant evidence will be brought to the attention of the tribunal, it can result in a considerable increase in the cost of the proceedings, as well as their length.

In civil law countries, the approach is often different. Some common law systems (e.g. England) are also moving closer to this approach. In these systems, the parties produce those documents upon which they intend to rely, whilst leaving it open to a party to apply to the tribunal for an order that the other party produce specific, identified documents which are in its possession which have not been produced voluntarily. Consequently, a party may be relieved of the obligation to produce embarrassing documents which have not been identified by the other side and the proceedings are generally less complex and costly.

Where the parties to an arbitration are from different legal backgrounds, it is necessary to come to some form of compromise. Article 3 of the IBA Rules of Evidence provides for a limited form of disclosure which is closer to that found in civil law countries. It adopts a system whereby a party can request identified documents, giving a description of why the requested documents are relevant and material to the outcome of the case and stating (a) that the requested documents are not in the possession, custody or control of the requesting party and (b) why the requesting party assumes that they are in the possession custody or control of his opponent.

Even when both parties are from a common law background, they should bear in mind that it is not the purpose of international arbitration proceedings simply to copy the procedures used in the state courts.

One of the advantages of arbitration is that the parties are free to choose the procedure which results in the most efficient conduct of the arbitration whilst still allowing the tribunal to establish the facts. They should, therefore, consider carefully whether disclosure is appropriate or whether it should be limited to particular classes of documents or issues. This is a matter which should be dealt with at the preliminary meeting (see pages 93–94 above). If the parties are unable to agree, the tribunal should give a direction on the matter.

Sometimes documents relevant to the issues in the arbitration are in the possession of third parties (i.e. those who are not parties to the arbitration proceedings). Except in arbitrations conducted in the United States, a tribunal generally does not have the power (which a state court would have) to compel a third party to produce documents. An application must therefore be made to the courts of the state in which the documents are to be found for an order requiring production of them. Such applications will only be possible if permitted by the law of that state.

If many documents are being disclosed, it is important that they should be properly organised. If they are not, this will result in lengthy proceedings and the arbitrators will find it difficult to follow the submissions on the evidence. The parties should attempt to agree on the organisation of the documents. To the extent that they cannot do so, directions should be sought from the tribunal.

Witnesses

Parties may agree that an arbitration is to proceed on the basis of the evidence contained in documents alone. This is often so in the case of commodity arbitrations. However, parties usually wish to bring to the attention of the tribunal a witness's evidence on the issues of fact. As with documents, witnesses fall into two principal categories:

(a) Witnesses of fact (i.e. witnesses who testify as to what they heard or saw).
(b) Opinion, or expert witnesses, who give evidence on matters which require expert analysis. For example, in order to establish negligence in a claim that an architect negligently designed a building, it is necessary to produce evidence from an expert (e.g. an experienced architect) who can consider the facts and express an opinion on whether or not the architect was negligent. Special considerations apply to expert witnesses, which are discussed in the next section.

As with documents, the approach to witnesses differs according to the legal background of the parties. Oral evidence assumes particular significance in the state courts of common law countries, where great importance is attached to the cross-examination (i.e. to subject the witness to rigorous and searching questioning) of the witnesses appearing on behalf of the other party. This is often referred to as the "adversarial" approach. The common law judge tends to leave the examination of witnesses to the parties. In civil law countries, the role of the judge is more active, taking a leading part in questioning witnesses (which is why the civil law approach is described as "inquisitorial"). The ability of the parties to cross-examine witnesses is restricted.

The practice of international commercial arbitration has seen a convergence of the systems. Arbitrators, even from common law backgrounds, are taking a more active and interventionist role with regard to evidence, but a degree of cross-examination of witnesses is generally permitted. Article 8(2) of the IBA Rules of Evidence allows for a party to question the witnesses provided by the other party or parties. It is now common for the parties to be required to exchange with each other a written statement of the evidence to be given by their witnesses. (Witness statements are provided for in Article 4 of the IBA Rules of Evidence.) Statements should be exchanged sufficiently in advance of the hearing that proper consideration can be given to the evidence by the opposing party. This may also help prompt settlement negotiations.

With the exchange of written witness statements, the common law practice of a party asking questions of its own witness at the hearing becomes redundant. The examination of witnesses therefore passes, at an early stage of the hearing, into the hands of the tribunal and the representative of the opposing party. Where cross-examination is permitted, it is usual for the party which has called the witness to be permitted to re-examine its witness (i.e. to ask questions to clear up any misunderstandings which may have been created in the course of cross-examination). It is becoming more common to limit the amount of time that may be taken up with cross-examination.

As noted above (page 99), the practice of some states prohibits a party from acting as a witness in support of his own case or prohibit a party's lawyer from interviewing witnesses or potential witnesses before the hearing. Where the parties find themselves subject to such restrictions, and to the extent permitted by the law applicable to the arbitration proceedings, they may wish to agree to free themselves of them. Articles 4(2) and (3) of the IBA Rules of Evidence provide that the parties will not be subject to these constraints.

Expert witnesses

The manner in which expert evidence is to be dealt with lies at the heart of many heated debates in international arbitration. In common law countries it is customary for each of the parties to appoint its own expert witness (or witnesses, where more than one discipline is involved) to provide an opinion for the tribunal. These witnesses are supposed to be independent of the parties, but opponents of the system point out that this independence is often more apparent than real (the witnesses' fees are paid by the party) and that the witnesses can end up acting as advocates for the cause of those employing them.

In civil law countries an expert (often selected from a court-approved panel) is often appointed to prepare a report for the tribunal and the parties. Opponents of this system point out that it is for the tribunal to decide all matters in issue between the parties and that it must not delegate that task to anyone else. Indeed, it sometimes does happen that a tribunal simply accepts the opinion of a tribunal-appointed expert, rather than evaluating it and then deciding whether to accept or reject it. Where this happens, an important element of the dispute may effectively be decided by someone who was not within the contemplation of the parties at the time the proceedings were commenced. A party may feel even more aggrieved if it has gone to great lengths to ensure that an appropriate tribunal has been appointed to decide the dispute.

Again, a convergence of the two systems is noticeable in international arbitration. Common features of the AAA/ICDR's International Arbitration Rules (Article 22), the LCIA Arbitration Rules (Article 21), the UNCITRAL Arbitration Rules (Article 27) and the UNCITRAL Model Law (Article 26) are that:

(a) the tribunal may appoint experts to report to it and to the parties;

(b) the parties may question the experts at a hearing; and

(c) the parties may present their own expert witnesses at the hearing.

The ICC Arbitration Rules only refer to tribunal-appointed experts (Article 20(4)), but it is not uncommon to come across party-appointed experts in ICC arbitrations.

In every case it is important to ensure that the mission of the expert is clearly spelt out. In the case of a tribunal-appointed expert, this may be done by agreement, failing which it must be dealt with by the tribunal. A timetable for the preparation of the tribunal expert's report must be established so as to give the parties sufficient time to consider the report before the hearing and to appoint their own experts, if they think that that is appropriate and such appointment is permitted.

Where experts are to be appointed by the parties, the timetable for the giving of their evidence and the manner in which it is to be given must also be established. The best time to do this is at a preliminary meeting. There are many ways of proceeding with regard to expert evidence, depending on the nature of the case, as the following two examples show.

(a) The parties should exchange their experts' reports and do so well before the hearing. Following exchange the experts should meet in an attempt to agree on issues leaving only those issues on which they disagree to be dealt with at the hearing.

(b) Where the experts have to deal with a large number of issues, it may be appropriate for their evidence to be given issue by issue. In other words, the tribunal will hear the evidence of both experts on one issue before moving on to deal with the next issue. Such a procedure will make it much easier for the tribunal to follow and evaluate the experts' evidence.

THE HEARING

Unless it is excluded in the arbitration agreement, the parties generally have a right to oral hearings on the issues. They may have hearings on:

(a) preliminary issues, such as whether or not a claim falls within the scope of the tribunal's jurisdiction; and

(b) the main substantive issues between them.

The basic procedure can be the same for both types of hearing, though in the case of the former, the tribunal may not have much by way of evidence before it.

The background of the parties (and the tribunal) will, yet again, have an influence on the way they approach hearings. It has already been seen in the section on evidence (pages 99–104) that the civil law tradition is inquisitorial, whereas that of the common law is adversarial. However, as already mentioned, the parties to an arbitration need not feel bound to follow the approach adopted by the courts in their respective states. Subject to any mandatory rules of the law applicable to the arbitration proceedings, the parties can agree on the procedure for hearings (which may also include agreeing on institutional rules containing provisions on procedure). In the absence of agreement, the tribunal will give directions and, again, the tribunal need not be constrained by the approach adopted by any particular jurisdiction.

At the hearing the various elements of the proceedings (such as submissions and documentary and oral evidence) come together. If the hearing is to be conducted efficiently, it is important that the parties should know what is likely to be expected of them at the hearing so that they can prepare accordingly. Accordingly, the conduct of the hearing should ideally be discussed and decided at the preliminary meeting.

Representation at hearings

The parties are usually entitled to be represented at hearings by a lawyer. Some countries, such as Chile, do not allow direct representation by foreign lawyers in arbitrations conducted in their territories. It was only in September 1996 that Japan amended its laws to allow foreign lawyers to represent their clients in international arbitrations conducted in Japan. The position in the relevant state should be checked. Singapore, for example, further liberalised its rules in 2004.

Arrangements for hearings

The manner in which the arrangements for the hearing are made will depend on whether or not the arbitration is a fully administered institutional arbitration (see page 31 above). If so, the institution may be able to assist in making the arrangements. In other cases it is up to the parties to do so, with the principal responsibility falling on the claimant.

The hearing will be held at the place agreed on by the parties or, failing agreement, at the place directed by the tribunal. A venue (e.g. a hotel or conference centre in the agreed place) will only be suitable if it has adequate space for everyone who is to attend, together with all their documents and their information technology resources. It should do so in sufficient comfort to enable them to concentrate on the task in hand. The venue should also have available rooms in which the parties can meet privately with their legal advisers, or with each other if settlement remains a possibility. Finally, support services should not be overlooked. In any substantial arbitration, there may be a need for secretarial and computer support and photocopying services.

Unless the parties have agreed otherwise, hearings will be held in private.

The order of proceedings at the hearing

The party which has the principal burden to discharge in establishing its case will usually open the proceedings. At the main substantive hearing this will almost always be the claimant. However, at hearings on preliminary issues, it may be the respondent (as when the respondent has made an application to have a claim dismissed for being outside the scope of the arbitrator's jurisdiction).

A traditional common law approach in state courts is that the party which opens makes an opening statement to the tribunal. This is followed by the evidence of the witnesses for that party and their cross-examination. The other party's opening statement and evidence then follow. The opening party may conclude the hearing with a reply.

Notwithstanding this, it is becoming more common for both parties in international arbitrations to make their opening statements at the beginning of the hearing and then follow up with the evidence.

Opening statements should not be lengthy because parties are usually encouraged to provide the arbitral tribunal with full written submissions in advance of the hearing.

Once the evidence has been concluded, the parties should each have an opportunity to make submissions to the tribunal by way of reply on matters arising in the course of the hearing.

Transcripts

It may be appropriate to arrange for a transcript to be made of the hearing. Modern technology is now such that in many parts of the world a transcript may be produced in real time, and displayed on screens in the hearing room, or at least made available later the same day. This can be of great help to both the tribunal and the parties in their attempts to keep track of the oral arguments and evidence given by witnesses. However, the cost of providing transcripts may be high and has to be borne by the parties. A transcript is therefore usually only appropriate in cases in which large amounts are at stake and which turn on a substantial amount of disputed oral evidence.

THE USE OF INFORMATION TECHNOLOGY IN ARBITRATION

Email is just one of the ways in which information technology can be used in international arbitration. Some of the other ways in which technology can be used as a tool in arbitration are discussed briefly below.

(a) The parties may use various media to exchange data. For example, submissions, witness statements and documentary evidence can all be sent to the other party and the tribunal electronically, or made available by a dedicated extranet, or electronic data room. There are a number of technical issues which would need to be considered here, including the formats of the data, which would have to be agreed by the parties in advance.

(b) If documents (e.g. submissions and evidence) are to be made available by a secure website to which the parties and the tribunal can be given access, security measures will be needed to protect against unauthorised access or improper monitoring of access.

(c) Document organisation and analysis can be easier and quicker than with paper documents: a keyword search enables users to locate particular documents, or even particular clauses within documents, in a relatively short time. However, whilst such systems can produce significant costs savings once they have been set up, the cost of putting them into place can be very high. As such, it may be that such document management systems will only be considered in higher value cases.

(d) In cases where the participants in the arbitration are in different parts of the world, video-conferencing can be used to enable parties to hold face-to-face discussions whilst in distant physical locations. Video-conferencing may not always be a desirable substitute for physical presence at a hearing – there may be concerns as to the integrity of the process, e.g. the sudden interruption of the video-link at a difficult point in a witness's cross-examination, or the perception that a person "off camera" is giving instructions to a witness giving evidence by video-link. (This concern is easily overcome by having a local independent agent to monitor the process.) However, video-conferencing may be a cost-effective way to conduct preliminary meetings and other procedural hearings.

(e) As mentioned on page 106 above, a transcript of the proceedings can be useful during an arbitration hearing. Such transcripts were typically produced on disk and/or in hard copy. However, it is possible to arrange electronic transcripts which enable participants in the arbitration, both in the hearing room and beyond (via the internet), to view a simultaneous transcript on-screen. In some cases, those present in the hearing room can annotate the transcript and communicate with others outside the room. This electronic transcript facility is particularly useful where the language of the arbitration is not the first language of some of the participants.

Whilst the use of information technology can undoubtedly enhance the arbitral process, whether or not a particular tool will be appropriate will depend on the circumstances of each case. Apart from the technical issues which must be considered, matters such as the IT literacy of the tribunal and what the tribunal should do if one party objects to the use of IT proposed by the other party may also need to be addressed. With regard to the latter, the tribunal must bear in mind that most arbitral laws and rules (institutional and non-institutional) require the parties to be treated equally and to have a full opportunity to present their case.

FAILURE BY ONE PARTY TO PARTICIPATE

The fact that the parties have entered into an arbitration agreement does not necessarily mean that they will ultimately feel bound to comply with the procedures that it contains. The nature of the dispute between them may be such that the parties, or at least one of them, are far less co-operative than was previously the case. That may result in one of the parties failing to participate at all, especially if it looks as if the arbitration may not be going in its favour. Alternatively, an unsuccessful party may also fail to participate when the successful party comes to enforce the award. What happens, procedurally, when a party fails to participate?

The arbitration agreement

Reference should first be made to the arbitration agreement between the parties. A well drafted non-institutional arbitration agreement will deal with the problem by permitting the tribunal to continue with the arbitration and make an award in spite of one party's failure to co-operate (see, for example, paragraph 11 in Appendix 6 and Article 28 of the UNCITRAL Arbitration Rules). The arbitration rules of the leading arbitration institutions also contain similar provisions (see Article 15(8) of the LCIA Arbitration Rules, Article 21(2) of the ICC Arbitration Rules and Article 23 of the AAA/ICDR International Arbitration Rules).

The law applicable to the arbitration proceedings

If the point is not covered in the arbitration agreement, or in any rules referred to in that agreement, one must have regard to the law applicable to the arbitration proceedings. Such laws vary a great deal. Section 41 of the English Arbitration Act 1996 makes provision for an arbitrator to decide the dispute in the absence of one of the parties. Article 25 of the UNCITRAL Model Law provides that if any party fails to appear at a hearing or to produce documentary evidence, the tribunal may continue the proceedings and make the award on the evidence before it.

If neither the arbitration agreement nor the law applicable to the arbitration proceedings contains an appropriate provision there is a risk that the arbitration will be brought to a standstill, or that any award made by the tribunal will be open to attack at the enforcement stage (though an attack which will not always be fatal).

Ex parte hearings

Hearings which are conducted in the absence of one of the parties are often referred to as "*ex parte*" or "without notice" hearings. Even if a respondent refuses to participate any further in an arbitration, an award in favour of the claimant should not be given as a matter of course. A claimant should still be required to establish its case in an *ex parte* hearing by showing that its case is soundly based in law and there is evidence to support the essential facts (this is reflected in the language of Article 25 of the UNCITRAL Model Law). This is not least because a reasoned award is necessary for it to be valid and enforceable. The claimant's task will, of course, be made much easier if the respondent has deprived itself of the opportunity of contesting those facts at a hearing.

In the unusual event that it is the claimant which refuses to continue with the arbitration, the respondent will normally be entitled to an award in its favour on the issues raised in the claimant's claim and an order terminating the arbitration (see Article 28(1) of the UNCITRAL Arbitration Rules), though it must still establish to the satisfaction of the tribunal any counter-claim which it may have.

A controversial proposal that UNCITRAL has been considering is to make provision for *ex parte* applications to an arbitral tribunal for interim measures of protection, which could then be enforced by state courts.

CHAPTER 8

AWARDS

INTRODUCTION

Unless a settlement is reached, the objective in any arbitration is a decision of an arbitral tribunal contained in a valid and enforceable award. There is no definition of the term "award" contained in any of the international conventions dealing with arbitration.

In some arbitrations there is only one decision by the arbitral tribunal contained in a single award. In most arbitrations, however, the tribunal will produce a number of decisions and directions at various stages. These might include decisions on challenges to its jurisdiction, directions as to the conduct of the arbitration, decisions on some of the claims submitted to arbitration before decisions on others, as well as decisions disposing of the totality of the matters in dispute. Not all of these decisions are "awards".

Making the correct distinction between those decisions which are awards and those which are not is not merely an academic exercise. "Awards" are decisions of the tribunal which finally dispose of an issue, or issues, between the parties and which will be given recognition and effect by state courts (at least in any state with a developed system of arbitration law). Decisions and directions which relate only to procedural matters (such as the timetable for submissions, the nature and extent of disclosure of documents, etc) are not properly described as "awards". The parties are expected to abide by any procedural order or directions but generally it is for the tribunal to decide upon the consequences of that failure (in the light of the arbitration agreement, the relevant arbitration rules and the law applicable to the arbitration proceedings).

This chapter will review the various types of award; the remedies which may be included in an award; issues affecting the validity of an award; and, finally, the consequences of an invalid award.

TYPES OF AWARD

The principal types of award include the following:

(a) provisional;
(b) interim;
(c) partial;

(d) final;

(e) consent;

(f) default.

The names used for different types of awards should be regarded as useful guides rather than definitive categorisations. The key factors in considering any award are: does the award deal with the substantive matters at issue between the parties; is the award reversible; does the award finally deal with all substantive matters at issue between the parties or only some of these issues.

Provisional awards

The arbitration laws of a number of states (see, for example, section 39 of the English Arbitration Act 1996) and the rules of a number of arbitral institutions (see, for example, Article 25 of the LCIA Arbitration Rules), as well as Article 26 of the UNCITRAL Arbitration Rules provide that the parties can agree that the arbitral tribunal should have the power to order on a provisional basis any relief which it would have power to grant in a final award. Provisional awards may be useful where it is necessary to protect or preserve property, to order provisional payments in industries where cash flow is important or to provide security for costs. The key distinguishing feature of provisional awards is that, as the name suggests, they are reversible and in that sense do not finally dispose of any matter at issue between the parties.

Interim awards

An interim award is made during the course of an arbitration and usually does not address the substantive content of the dispute between the parties. It is however a final decision, but usually on procedural matters which need to be decided so that the arbitral tribunal can then address the substantive issues. For example, with the term used in this sense, interim awards will include awards addressing challenges to jurisdiction or providing a decision on the scope of the matters referred. In each case, at least one further award of the tribunal is needed to dispose finally of all issues between the parties (see for example Article 57 of the CIETAC Rules).

Partial awards

These are awards which finally deal with only some of the substantive matters at issue between the parties typically because matters are being dealt with in the proceedings in stages. For example, a partial award may require a payment to be made by one party to the other, either on account of damages to be assessed or following a decision on only a part of the claims raised before the tribunal.

Final awards

Final awards are awards which dispose of all of the issues in an arbitration (or all the remaining issues, if there has already been one or more partial awards) and which thereby conclude the function of the arbitral tribunal. A final award will be the last award of a tribunal.

Some confusion has been caused by the use of the word "final" to signify that an award finally disposes of the issues between the parties and that it is not subject to any review procedure. Finality, in this sense, was important in the context of proceedings for the enforcement of an award under the Geneva Convention of 1927 (Article 1(2)(d)) and is imposed by the rules of certain arbitral institutions (such as the ICC and the LCIA) and the UNCITRAL Arbitration Rules. Finality in this sense is not necessary for enforcement under the New York Convention, which simply requires that the award should be "binding" on the parties (see Article V(1)(e)). Accordingly, an interim award and a partial award can be enforced under the New York Convention.

Consent awards

Consent awards are those made with the consent of the parties following a settlement of their dispute. Disputes submitted to arbitration are often settled on the basis that receipt of an all-inclusive payment is made a condition for the termination of the arbitration proceedings. In such cases, an award terminating the arbitration is not necessary. There may, however, be occasions when a settlement is achieved, but the paying party lacks the means to make an immediate payment and it is agreed that payment can be made later, or by instalments. If the arbitration is discontinued without an award, the obligation of the paying party to honour the settlement agreement could only be enforced by commencing fresh proceedings based on the settlement agreement. This unsatisfactory situation can be avoided by incorporating the terms of the settlement in a consent award. Enforcement of the terms of settlement can then be achieved by enforcing the consent award.

Default awards

A default award is an award made in proceedings where one of the parties (usually the respondent) has refused to participate. Such awards are generally regarded as valid, provided that the absent party has been given a full opportunity to present its case and that the award amounts to a proper determination after the tribunal has evaluated the submissions and evidence provided by the party which did participate in the proceedings.

REMEDIES WHICH MAY BE INCLUDED IN AN AWARD

There are no universal rules determining the remedies available in an international arbitration. In the case of each dispute, the remedies to be included in an award need to be considered in the light of:

(a) the arbitration agreement, including any rules the parties have agreed should apply to the arbitration;

(b) the law applicable to the substance of the dispute; and
(c) the law applicable to the arbitration proceedings.

The remedies available in an international arbitration award include those set out below, although an order for the payment of money, declarations and interest are probably the most common remedies.

Order for the payment of money

An order for the payment of money by one party to another is the most common remedy found in awards. The payment may represent compensation for losses suffered (damages) or the payment of a debt (e.g. money due under a contract).

Generally speaking, an arbitral tribunal will not make an award directing payment of money by way of instalments unless the parties have expressly so agreed. Many states specifically provide for an arbitral tribunal to make its award in a currency other than that of the state in which the arbitration takes place. In the absence of such provisions the tribunal will need the consent of the parties.

Declaratory relief

Parties, particularly those in continuing relationships, may wish to have their legal rights and obligations clearly established in an award. An arbitral tribunal may include a declaration as to the parties' rights and obligations or the meaning of a contract or part of one in its award. A declaratory award is capable of recognition in proceedings commenced in the same state as the arbitration, or elsewhere.

Interest

The law and practice relating to the award of interest is a particularly difficult area. The law of some (notably Islamic) states forbids the award of interest, the law of some other states permits it and the law of a third group requires it. German law, for example, specifically provides that an arbitral tribunal must award interest according to defined rules. Accordingly there is no common international approach to the issue of whether arbitrators should award interest and the principles to be followed if interest is to be awarded.

To complicate matters further, the law of some states views the award of interest as essentially a procedural matter, while others regard it as a substantive issue. This distinction is important because it will impact on the determination of the law governing the award of interest. For example, if the award of interest is viewed as a substantive matter by the arbitration law of the seat, then the provisions of the law applicable to the substance of the dispute relating to the award of interest will apply.

Provisions relating to the award of interest may be found in the arbitration agreement itself (including any institutional rules to be applied). This is the best point from which to start when trying to establish whether or not, and in what manner, interest may be awarded. If forbidden to award interest by the law applicable to the arbitration agreement, the arbitral tribunal should not do it. If it were to do so, enforcement of the award, or at least that part of it which deals with interest, could be resisted (see Article V(1)(c) of the New York Convention).

If there is nothing in the arbitration agreement, provisions relating to the award of interest may also be found in the law applicable to:

(a) the substance of the dispute,
(b) the arbitration proceedings (i.e. the arbitration law of the seat), and/or
(c) the enforcement of an award made in another state.

The tribunal will have to consider the relevant conflict of law rules (see pages 12–17 above) when deciding which, if any, of the provisions on interest contained in the law applicable to the dispute or the law of the seat of the arbitration will apply. It is also important to consider the impact of the law of the state where enforcement of the award is sought. For example, if a claimant attempts to enforce an award which includes interest in a country which prohibits or treats as usurious the award of interest this may provide a ground for refusing enforcement (Article V(2)(b) of the New York Convention).

Specific performance

A party to an arbitration may request that the arbitral tribunal order its opponent to perform certain obligations. The difficulty with such an order is that it will depend, for its enforcement, on the assistance of state courts. Courts in a number of states, such as England, are prepared to provide such assistance, provided that the parties have not, in their agreement, deprived the arbitral tribunal of the power to order specific performance. Conversely, the courts of some other states will assist only if the parties have expressly agreed to confer such a power on the arbitral tribunal.

Injunction

Under the laws of many states, an arbitral tribunal has the power to grant relief by way of injunction. This power can, however, be illusory because any injunction can (in most states) only be enforced with assistance of the state courts which can take time even in urgent cases. Injunctions, particularly interim injunctions intended to prevent assets from being dissipated or to preserve property, will often depend for their effect on being obtained speedily. This may sometimes be without the opponent's knowledge. It may therefore be preferable to make such applications directly to a state court if that is possible. The courts of most states will accept jurisdiction in respect of such applications. The UNCITRAL Arbitration Rules and the rules of most arbitration institutions permit such applications to state courts, before or during the arbitration, by providing that they are not to be deemed incompatible with the agreement to arbitrate, and are not a waiver of that agreement.

Rectification

Parties to an agreement sometimes fail accurately to record what has been agreed and one of the parties subsequently attempts to exploit the discrepancy. An arbitral tribunal may correct an agreement to reflect what was actually agreed and enforce the "rectified" agreement, provided that the parties have given such a tribunal the power to do so. Whether the parties have done so is a question of interpretation of the arbitration agreement. In England, the power to rectify a contract is expressly conferred on a tribunal by statute (section 48(5) of the Arbitration Act 1996).

Punitive damages

These are damages awarded over and above the damages required to compensate an injured party for its loss. They are particularly relevant in the context of arbitrations conducted in the USA. In the US case of *Mastrobuono* v. *Shearson Lehman Hutton Inc.* (1995) it was held that the arbitrators were authorised to award punitive damages unless the parties had explicitly withdrawn that power in the arbitration agreement (although note that Article 28(5) of the AAA/ICDR International Arbitration Rules expressly withdraws the power). By contrast, punitive damages are a much rarer phenomenon in other states where, if they are available at all, it is only in circumstances akin to fraud. Significant problems can arise in international arbitrations if enforcement of an award containing punitive damages is sought in a state which for public policy grounds does not permit punitive damages.

Costs

The word "costs" is used generally to describe all types of costs incurred in an arbitration. However, a more precise distinction should be drawn between:

(a) *the costs of the arbitration*: these include the arbitrator's fees, the hire of the venue and the administrative costs of any institution which might have been involved; and

(b) *the costs of the parties*: these include the fees and disbursements of the parties' lawyers and experts, and witness expenses – which do not include the cost of the time which a party, or the members of its staff, have had to devote to the arbitration (though in some cases this cost may be recoverable in the award as an item of special damage).

When considering the rules regarding the costs of an arbitration there are two important sources to consider:

(a) the provisions of the arbitration agreement (including any applicable rules referred to in it) relating to costs; and

(b) since the award of costs is essentially a procedural matter, the provisions on costs in the arbitration law of the seat.

The rules of the principal arbitration institutions such as the AAA/ICDR, the ICC and the LCIA, as well as the UNCITRAL Arbitration Rules, contain specific provisions requiring the arbitral tribunal to fix the costs of the arbitration. They either require or empower a tribunal to apportion the costs as between the parties. In apportioning costs the arbitral tribunal has a broad discretion. There is no universally established practice as to the way that discretion should be exercised, but the tribunal will be influenced by matters such as the extent to which the parties have succeeded on the principal issues and the conduct of the parties during the arbitration (i.e. if a party has been responsible for unnecessarily complicating or extending the proceedings, that may be reflected in the award on costs).

Where the arbitration agreement (and any arbitration rules referred to in it) is silent on the question of costs, one must look to the provisions of the law applicable to the arbitration proceedings. Such provisions vary from state to state. A tribunal will usually have a discretion as to how costs are to be awarded, although there is little uniformity as to the way in which the discretion is to be exercised.

VALIDITY OF THE AWARD

An award which is not valid (i.e. at the seat of the arbitration) is not normally capable of recognition or enforcement (save in the rather unusual circumstances of a case such as the *Hilmarton* case in which the French Cour de Cassation recognised a Swiss award which had been declared invalid by the Swiss courts). To be recognised and enforced an award must be valid but this does not necessarily mean that all valid awards will be recognised and enforced, particularly where recognition and enforcement is sought in another state (see pages 130–132 below, relating to the defences available on an application for recognition and enforcement).

The validity of an award depends on the provisions of:

(a) the arbitration agreement (including any applicable rules), and

(b) the law of the seat of the arbitration.

Such provisions usually address both the form and the content of the award.

As to "form", most applicable arbitration laws and rules require that an award should, at least:

(a) be in writing,
(b) state the reasons upon which it is based (unless the parties have agreed that it should not),
(c) state its date,
(d) state the place where it was made, or deemed to be made, i.e. the seat of the arbitration, and
(e) be signed by the members of the tribunal. If one member of a three-person tribunal is not in agreement with the decision of the other two and refuses to sign the award, the rules of the principal arbitration institutions and the UNCITRAL Arbitration Rules do not allow this to detract from the validity of the award.

In every case the relevant provisions should be checked to see what is required.

As to "content", an award must:

(a) be the product of an arbitration conducted in accordance with the requirements of the arbitration agreement, the mandatory requirements of the law of the seat of the arbitration and with due regard to the principle of equality of treatment of the parties;
(b) deal only with those matters which the parties have agreed to refer to arbitration. For example, if a submission to arbitration is expressly limited to the issue of whether or not a buyer was entitled to reject allegedly defective goods, the award should not include an award of damages. If it did, it would take the award beyond the scope of the submission to arbitration;
(c) where it is a "final" award, it should deal with all the matters which have been referred to arbitration, except to the extent that they have already been finally dealt with in any prior award;
(d) dispose of the issues finally (in the sense given at page 113 above), clearly and unambiguously;
(e) set out the reasons for the tribunal's decision, unless:
     (i)   the parties have agreed otherwise, or
     (ii) the award is a consent award, or
     (iii) the law of the seat of the arbitration does not require it.

The practice of arbitrators in giving reasons varies enormously and it is often difficult to establish if the reasons given are sufficient. Some arbitrators make a virtue of brevity, whilst others set out their reasoning in great detail. The essential feature of reasons is that they should enable anyone reading the award to ascertain how the arbitral tribunal has reached its decision. They should, therefore, at least include a reference to all the issues raised by the parties, all findings of fact relevant to those issues and an explanation of how the tribunal came to its decision on the legal issues.

A further requirement which may have to be complied with to achieve a valid award is to ensure the award is made within any time limit provided for in the arbitration agreement or the arbitration law of the seat. If the tribunal fails to make the award within a prescribed time limit, its authority is terminated and it cannot make a valid award.

Whilst time limits for the making of awards are to be found in a number of state arbitration laws and in the rules of institutions such as the ICC, they can usually be extended by agreement of the parties or at the request of the arbitral tribunal. Parties must give careful attention to the time limits and ensure that any extensions required are obtained.

OTHER REQUIREMENTS FOR ENFORCEMENT

There are some further requirements which may (and in the case of communication to the parties, will) have to be observed before an award made by a tribunal can be enforced.

Review

The rules of the ICC require that there be scrutiny of the draft award by the ICC's International Court of Arbitration so that it can ensure that the award is valid as to its form and to give it the opportunity to draw to the attention of the tribunal any substantive points which may be of concern. The AAA/ICDR and the LCIA rules make no such provision for scrutiny of the award.

Communication

The award must be communicated to the parties.

In the case of institutional arbitration, the communication of the award and the payment of the tribunal's fees will be dealt with in accordance with the institution's rules.

In a non-institutional (i.e. *ad hoc*) arbitration, where all of the tribunal's fees have been paid by the parties it will do this simply by sending a copy of the award to each of the parties. If, however, the fees have not been paid at the time of the award the tribunal will notify the parties that the award is available for collection once the outstanding fees have been paid. If a party anticipates an unfavourable award and refuses to pay its share of the tribunal's fees, the other party will have to pay them in order to obtain the award (the fees will usually be recoverable under the award).

The date on which the award is communicated is important because it will generally determine the commencement of time limits for the making of any available appeal. Communication is usually regarded as taking place when the party receives a copy of the award, not when it is notified that it is available for collection. If there is likely to be any delay in collecting the award, the arbitration law of the seat should be checked on this point.

Registration or deposit

The registration or deposit of an award is sometimes required as a condition for its validity or as a necessary preliminary to its enforcement either in the state in which it has been made or, in some cases, in a foreign state. The relevant laws should in each case be checked.

CONSEQUENCES OF INVALIDITY

Two important points have already been made:

(a) An invalid award is not capable of recognition or enforcement.
(b) A final award concludes the function of the arbitral tribunal (or, as it is sometimes put, renders it *functus officio*), depriving it of any further jurisdiction over the dispute.

This might lead one to conclude that the making of an invalid final award could be a catastrophe requiring the appointment of a new tribunal, and further hearings, to sort out such things as calculation errors or accidental omission. But this will not always be so. In each case the arbitration agreement (including the rules, if any, which the parties have agreed should apply to the arbitration), as well as the arbitration law of the seat, must be examined.

The rules of most institutions permit the correction of minor slips and errors of computation. The rules of the LCIA and the UNCITRAL Arbitration Rules go further by permitting the tribunal to make an additional award to deal with issues raised in the arbitration but not dealt with in the award.

The relevant arbitration law of the seat applicable to the arbitration proceedings will also normally permit the correction of slips and may, particularly in the case of laws based on the UNCITRAL Model Law, also permit an additional award to be made to deal with an omitted issue. Where a state court has found that an award suffers from a remediable defect, the Model Law allows the court to remit the award to the arbitral tribunal to cure the defect.

CHAPTER 9

RECOGNITION OR ENFORCEMENT
OF AWARDS

AFTER THE AWARD

Having received an award made in its favour, the "successful" party in arbitration can expect one of three things to happen:

(a) the award is honoured – for example, the other party
    (i) pays the successful party the amounts awarded to it without delay, or
    (ii) accepts any declarations made in the award and acts in accordance with them; or
(b) the other party effectively ignores the award but takes no active steps to resist it; or
(c) the other party actively challenges the award and/or resists any attempt by the "successful" party to have the award recognised or enforced.

This chapter examines what a "successful" party in situation (b) or (c) might do to compel the other party to give effect to the award. In contrast, the next chapter looks at how a party may actively challenge an award (in its entirety or in part) with a view to the award being modified or set aside altogether.

RECOGNITION OR ENFORCEMENT

Faced with a recalcitrant opponent, a "successful" party may seek the assistance of the state courts to compel its opponent to give effect to the award. In doing so, the "successful" party will ask the courts either to "recognise" or to "recognise and enforce" the award.

"Recognition" without subsequent enforcement may be sought as a defensive measure when a party wishes to rely on the award to defeat claims brought against it in other proceedings (whether actual or anticipated) which are unconnected to the arbitration – for example, if the award has already finally determined an issue raised in the other proceedings, the state court may be asked to accept the award of the tribunal as binding on the parties with regard to the issues covered by it, and to render a judgment which is consistent with the arbitral award.

An award is "enforced" when a state court assists in compelling the recalcitrant party to comply with the terms of the award, for example, by seizing that party's assets. However, before a court can enforce an award, the award may need to be "recognised" by the court in the sense that the court needs to accept that the decision of the tribunal is valid and that it is binding on the parties. In this way, "recognition" of an award is often a necessary precursor to commencing enforcement proceedings.

Domestic and foreign awards

Different (through perhaps overlapping) procedures are available for the recognition and/or enforcement of "domestic" and "foreign" awards. For present purposes, a "domestic" award is one which is to be recognised and/or enforced in the state in which it was made whereas a "foreign" award is one in respect of which recognition and/or enforcement is sought in a state other than that in which it was made.

This begs the question: "Where is the award made?" This must be considered in the light of the law applicable in the state in which the application for recognition and/or enforcement is made, together with any rules which the parties have agreed should apply to the arbitration. A number of states treat an award as having been made in the country in which it was signed by the arbitrator. Thus, in an English case (*Hiscox* v. *Outhwaite* (1991) the effect of which has now been reversed by the Arbitration Act 1996) the English courts treated as "foreign" an award which had been signed in Paris, even though the entirety of the arbitration proceedings themselves had been conducted in England. In order to avoid such a haphazard result, some arbitration rules specify where the award is to be made. For example:

(a) the AAA/ICDR International Arbitration Rules provide that an award is made in the place specified in the award. That place must be the place of the arbitration itself (Article 27(3)), and

(b) the ICC Arbitration Rules provide that the award shall be deemed to be made at the place of the arbitration proceedings (Article 25(3)), i.e. the seat, even though meetings, hearings and deliberations may have taken place at other locations.

WHERE TO APPLY FOR RECOGNITION OR ENFORCEMENT

An application for recognition alone (i.e. without enforcement proceedings) will necessarily be brought in the courts of the state where the other proceedings have been commenced against the party who wishes to rely on the award as part of its defence. Occasionally (as in the *Hilmarton* case (see page 117 above) a party may include an application for recognition in proceedings for a pre-emptive declaration designed to frustrate any subsequent attempt by the other party to enforce an award dealing with related issues.

In the case of applications for enforcement, however, the "successful" party may have a choice of state courts. In such a case, the primary consideration will usually be the location of the assets against which enforcement is sought because a state court can assist only with the enforcement of an award against assets which are within the jurisdiction of that state court. Also, enforcement in one state may be easier and quicker than in another. Accordingly, before commencing any enforcement proceedings, it is worth the "successful" party investing some time and costs tracing the whereabouts of the recalcitrant party's assets in order to identify whether one or more states is likely to prove to be a more favourable (and effective) forum for enforcement.

Where assets are found in a number of separate states, a separate application for enforcement will be required for each state in which there are assets needed to meet the award. There are some countries, such as the United Kingdom and the United States of America, which are made up of a number of separate legal jurisdictions. Thus, for example, if the assets which are needed to satisfy the award are spread across both England and Scotland, the "successful" party will need to make two separate applications for enforcement, to the courts in England and to the courts in Scotland.

The location of assets is not, however, the only relevant factor. An application for the enforcement of a foreign award will not progress very far if the law of the state in which the assets are found does not provide for the enforcement of awards made in the state in which the award was made. Pressing ahead with such an application will simply be a waste of time and money. Thus, before making an application for enforcement of an award the "successful" party must:

(a) establish whether the state in which enforcement is sought is a party to the New York Convention. It will not be necessary that the state in which the award was made should also be a party to the Convention, provided that the state in which enforcement is sought has not availed itself of the "reciprocity reservation" (see column 1 of Appendix 1);

(b) where the New York Convention cannot be relied upon, find out whether there are any other conventions or bilateral treaties which may provide a remedy (see Chapter 2 above);

(c) in the event that there are no conventions or treaties that may be relied upon, look to the law of the state in which enforcement is sought to see whether, nevertheless, it provides for the enforcement of foreign awards. For example, in England, a foreign award may, with the permission of the High Court, be enforced in the same manner as a judgment of the courts (section 66 of the Arbitration Act 1996), or it may constitute the basis of an ordinary action in the English courts brought to enforce the obligations arising under the award.

Whether or not an enforcement convention or treaty applies, "public policy" considerations in the proposed state in which enforcement is sought can be a critical factor in choosing a forum for enforcement proceedings. For example:

(a) In France, a foreign award is enforceable, or will be recognised, if its existence is proved by the party relying on it and its enforcement, or recognition, is not manifestly contrary to international public policy (Article 1498 of the Code of Civil Procedure). As was demonstrated in the *Hilmarton* case (see page 117 above), the recognition of an award that has been set aside in the state courts of the seat of the arbitration does not run counter to French notions of international public policy. In this respect the French regime for recognition and enforcement is even more favourable for the successful party than that of the New York Convention.

(b) Similarly, in the United States of America, provided the award conforms to certain legal criteria in the state of enforcement, the courts are willing to exercise their discretion in favour of enforcing an award even if it has been annulled elsewhere. Thus, in the *Chromalloy* case (1999), US courts recognised and enforced an award that had been made in Egypt but annulled by the Egyptian courts, on the basis that it was valid and enforceable under the relevant US domestic law and that the Egyptian annulment was contrary to "US public policy in favour of final and binding arbitration of commercial disputes". However, in the *Baker Marine* case (1999), the US courts refused to enforce an award that had been made in Nigeria and annulled by the Nigerian courts, on the basis that the parties had agreed that their disputes and any associated arbitration would be governed by Nigerian law. Thus, US recognition of an award annulled in the country of origin is not automatic and, it seems, will be heavily influenced by US public policy of upholding party autonomy.

(c) Although Russia is a party to the New York Convention, in practical terms "successful" parties may find a Russian court outside Moscow reluctant to enforce a foreign award against a recalcitrant Russian entity based in the provinces, particularly if enforcement is sought against real (as opposed to monetary) assets and could have an adverse effect on the economy of a local Russian town or area.

In every case, advice should be taken at an early stage from lawyers with expertise in the state in which enforcement is likely to be sought. They should know whether or not a foreign award will be enforceable, and in what manner. They should also be able to advise on the current attitude of the local courts towards requests for enforcement of "foreign" arbitral awards and any particular features in the legal system of the state in question. For example, notwithstanding the fact that Bangladesh is a party to the New York Convention, it has yet to implement the legislation for obtaining enforcement of an award pursuant to that Convention.

PROCEDURE FOR RECOGNITION OR ENFORCEMENT

The procedure for the recognition and/or enforcement of an award is to be found in the detailed provisions of the law of the state in question. If the arbitral award is a "domestic" award, clearly no international conventions or treaties will be relevant. However, in some jurisdictions, such as France, special procedural rules may apply to the recognition and/or enforcement of awards that are made in arbitrations which are regarded as "international".

As the procedure for the recognition and/or enforcement of a foreign award turns on the requirements of the law of the particular state in which the application is made, it is inappropriate to attempt to deal with it in any detail. However, in general terms, where a state is a party to the New York Convention it undertakes:

(a) to recognise arbitral awards as binding and to enforce them in accordance with its rules of procedure, under the conditions laid down in the rest of the Convention, and

(b) not to impose substantially more onerous conditions or higher fees or charges for recognition or enforcement of awards covered by the Convention than are imposed on the recognition or enforcement of domestic awards (Article III). In fact, on a more positive note, the Convention allows the successful party to avail itself of any more favourable regime for recognition or enforcement which may exist in the state in which the application is made. (Article VII).

Furthermore, the requirements of the New York Convention for obtaining recognition and/or enforcement have been kept to the minimum. The party applying for recognition and/or enforcement merely has to supply the appropriate court with:

(a) the authenticated original award, or a certified copy of it, and

(b) the original arbitration agreement, or a certified copy of it (Article IV(1)).

Documents which have not been prepared in an official language of the state in which the application is made must be translated into that language.

TIME LIMITS

The law of the place where recognition and/or enforcement of an award is sought (or, occasionally, the enforcement convention or treaty relied upon) may contain time limits for the commencement of such proceedings. These require early attention with the assistance of lawyers having expertise in the relevant state.

CHAPTER 10

CHALLENGING OR RESISTING ENFORCEMENT OF AWARDS

THE OPTIONS

Having persevered with an arbitration through to the conclusion of the hearing and the issuing of the award, one or both parties may be dissatisfied with the outcome. If so, the dissatisfied party has a number of options:

(a) where the rules applicable to the arbitration provide for it, to make an appeal to the appellate authority specified in the rules; and/or

(b) to challenge the award in the courts of the place where it was made, i.e. the seat of the arbitration (to the extent permitted by the local law); and/or

(c) to resist recognition or enforcement of the award in a state other than that in which it was made; and/or

(d) using the threat of one or more of options (a), (b) and (c), to attempt to negotiate a settlement on more favourable terms than the arbitral award; or

(e) to accept the award and comply with it.

These options should not be regarded as mutually exclusive. Whereas options (d) and (e) are essentially driven by commercial considerations – for example, a continuing trade relationship – options (a), (b) and (c) are more likely to depend on a complicated interaction of commercial, practical and legal considerations. This chapter will review each of options (a), (b) and (c) with a view to providing an overview as to the circumstances in which they are available and when it might be appropriate to exercise them.

APPEAL PURSUANT TO THE RULES OF THE ARBITRATION

This option is rarely available because one of the primary objectives of most parties when agreeing to arbitration is for any dispute to be disposed of finally and expeditiously by the arbitration process itself, without further recourse to legal proceedings. Since the appeal process can defeat that objective, the parties to an arbitration agreement will frequently expressly exclude any rights of appeal (see page 30 above). Nevertheless, in the absence of any such exclusion, the arbitration rules of some bodies expressly provide for an appeal (e.g. the ICSID rules, which are dealt with in the next chapter and certain commodity arbitrations). In each case the relevant rules will have to be analysed to establish that the proposed appeal is one which the rules allow and to identify any time limits which must be observed. For example, awards in commodity arbitrations may be appealed as to their merits, whereas an ICSID award may only be appealed for procedural reasons.

CHALLENGE IN THE COURTS OF THE STATE WHERE THE AWARD WAS MADE ("DOMESTIC" AWARDS)

This option, as distinct from the next option, involves the "dissatisfied" party initiating some positive action in the form of mounting a challenge in the courts of the state where the award was made.

The scope for challenging a "domestic" award and the nature of the relief available will be governed by a combination of the following:

(a) the law of the state where the award was made and is being challenged;
(b) the terms of the arbitration agreement (i.e. whether there are any limitations which may have been agreed by the parties – such as the exclusion of a right of appeal – and which are not contrary to any of the mandatory provisions of the law of the relevant state); and
(c) the nature of the alleged defect in the award.

Nature of relief

Ordinarily, the best that a "dissatisfied" party challenging the award can hope for is to have the award set aside, because an award that has been set aside is usually unenforceable. However, even if the award is not set aside, a "dissatisfied" party may obtain suitable relief if the court modifies or "varies" the award so that it is less objectionable, or returns or "remits" the award to the arbitral tribunal with instructions that it is to revise the award in a manner that will exclude the offending part.

Scope for challenging a "domestic" award

The basis on which a "domestic" award may be challenged in the state courts will be set out in the detailed provisions of the law of that state, but can be limited further by the terms of the parties' arbitration agreement. The law will not only differ considerably from one state to the next, but also from one arbitration agreement to another. For example:

(a) Those states which have adopted the UNCITRAL Model Law will only permit an application for setting aside an award and such applications are relatively rarely successful. In appropriate circumstances that application may be suspended to allow the award to be remitted to the tribunal so that it may take such steps as may be necessary to eliminate the grounds for setting aside. This might be appropriate, for example, where fresh evidence is discovered after the award has been made, which might have affected the decision of the tribunal if it had been produced at the hearing. The UNCITRAL Model Law makes no reference to an appeal on the merits of the award.

(b) Article 190 of the Swiss Private International Law Act of 1987 also only provides for an award to be set aside. Note that under Article 192 of the same Act, the right to apply to set aside can be excluded by express written agreement if the parties have no domicile, residence or business in Switzerland. A similar right to opt out was previously provided for in Belgian legislation.

(c) English law permits an appeal to the courts, albeit within narrowly defined circumstances. However, the parties' arbitration agreement may further limit the scope for challenging an award in that the parties can exclude the right to appeal on a question of law arising out of the award (section 69 of the Arbitration Act 1996). The other rights of appeal – based on challenges to the jurisdiction of the tribunal or the procedure of the arbitration (sections 67 and 68 of the Arbitration Act 1996 respectively) – are mandatory so that any attempt by the parties to exclude them by agreement will be void. If a challenge is successful, the English courts have power to vary or set aside the award, or to remit it for reconsideration by the arbitral tribunal.

Clearly, the diversity in the grounds on which an application to set aside or remit an award may be made is such that it is not practical to summarise all of them here. However, because of the widespread adoption of the UNCITRAL Model Law and because the grounds it prescribes are almost identical to the defences to an application for enforcement of a "foreign" award that are available under the New York Convention (under which many foreign awards are enforced), the summary on page 130 below ought to provide a helpful starting point in most cases. Significantly, the grounds are not mutually exclusive and a dissatisfied party may rely on such one or more of them as may be available.

Timing

A dissatisfied party who wishes to challenge an award will need to act quickly for a number of reasons. First, the time limits within which challenges must be made are usually short. Secondly, if the dissatisfied party is also the more unsuccessful party, any scent of undue reluctance on its party may provoke a "successful" party, anxious to enjoy the fruits of its victory, to press for compliance with the award by commencing enforcement proceedings. Thirdly, even though a second attempt at challenge may be available at the stage when recognition and/or enforcement as a "foreign" award is sought in another state, the grounds for challenge at that stage may be narrower. For example, the enforcement procedure available under the New York Convention does not permit any review of the merits.

RESISTING RECOGNITION AND/OR ENFORCEMENT OF A "FOREIGN" AWARD

As the word "resist" implies, this option merely requires the unsuccessful party to react to an application for recognition and/or enforcement of a "foreign" award. Until the application is made there is nothing that the unsuccessful party is required to do, although, if practical, it may choose to move its assets into a state in which the award is less easily enforceable – for example, one that is not a party to the New York Convention.

Application for recognition and/or enforcement

Depending on the local law, an application for recognition and/or enforcement of an award may be made:

(a) under the provisions of the New York Convention;

(b) under the provisions of some other convention or bilateral treaty;

(c) by commencing an action on the basis of the obligation created by the arbitral award; or

(d) by relying on such other means as may be available in the state where recognition and/or enforcement is sought (e.g. in England, enforcement in the same manner as a judgment of the courts, under section 66 of the Arbitration Act 1996).

The application will be served on the unsuccessful party, which will have an opportunity to raise any defences as to why the application should not be granted.

Defences under the New York Convention

The defences available to an unsuccessful party wishing to resist an application for recognition and/or enforcement of a "foreign" award will necessarily depend on the facts in each particular case and the basis upon which the application for recognition and/or enforcement has been made. Accordingly, it is not practical to address all of the possible defences available in this handbook. Instead, because applications for recognition and/or enforcement of a "foreign" award are most frequently made under the New York Convention, this section is limited to the defences available under that Convention.

In any event, because of the similarity between the provisions of the UNCI-TRAL Model Law (Articles 34 and 36) and Article V of the New York Convention, the New York Convention defences are also a useful indication of the types of defences which may be available when an application for recognition and/or enforcement is made by means other than under that Convention. Note, however, that the defences may not always apply – see the *Hilmarton* and *Chromalloy* cases (outlined at pages 117 and 124 above).

The defences to an application for recognition and/or enforcement under the New York Convention are listed in Article V. They are the only grounds on which recognition or enforcement may be refused under the Convention and are construed narrowly. Note, however, that the state court in which the application is made is not under an obligation to refuse recognition or enforcement if any such defence is raised. It simply has discretion to do so. The way in which that discretion is exercised is likely to be heavily influenced by public policy considerations in the state where enforcement is sought.

Broadly, the available defences fall into two groups. First, those defences which the unsuccessful party must raise and where the burden of proof rests with the unsuccesful party. Secondly, those defences which do not require the unsuccessful party to prove anything and which the state court can raise of its own motion (though an unsuccessful party would be well advised to draw them to the court's attention).

The first group includes defences based on:

(a) *The arbitration agreement*: An application for enforcement may be refused:
   (i) where the unsuccessful party can prove that the parties to the agreement were, under the law applicable to them, under some incapacity (which results in the arbitration agreement being invalid); or
   (ii) where the agreement is not valid under the law to which the parties have subjected it or, if they have made no indication in that respect, under the law of the state where the award was made (Article V(1)(a)).

(b) *Due process*: It is a defence if the unsuccessful party can prove that it was not given proper notice of the appointment of the arbitrator, or of the arbitration proceedings, or was otherwise unable to present its case (Article V(1)(b)).

(c) *Jurisdiction*: An application for enforcement may be refused if the unsuccessful party can prove that the award:
   (i) deals with a dispute not contemplated by or falling within the terms of the submission to arbitration, or
   (ii) contains decisions on matters beyond the scope of the submission to arbitration.

   Where, however, the decisions on matters which are beyond the scope of the submission to arbitration can be separated from those which are within the scope of the submission, then that part of the award which contains decisions on the matters within the scope of the submission may be recognised or enforced (Article V(1)(c)).

(d) *Procedure*: The appropriate procedure for the arbitration must have been followed. It is therefore a defence if the unsuccessful party can prove that:

(i) the composition of the arbitral tribunal, or

(ii) the arbitral procedure

was not in accordance with the agreement of the parties or, failing such agreement, not in accordance with the law of the seat of the arbitration (Article V(1)(d)).

(e) *The award*: An application for enforcement may be refused if the unsuccessful party can prove that the award:

(i) has not yet become binding on the parties; or

(ii) has been set aside or suspended by a competent authority of the state in which, or under the law of which, that award was made (Article V(1)(e)).

As regards the second group of defences, recognition or enforcement of an award may be refused if the competent authority in the state where the application for recognition enforcement has been made finds that:

(a) the subject-matter of the difference is not capable of settlement by arbitration under the law of that state; or

(b) recognition or enforcement of the award would be contrary to the public policy of that state. (Article V(2).)

Reservations

In addition to the list of defences permitted by the New York Convention, the unsuccessful party may also be able to resist enforcement of a foreign award by relying on the "commercial" and/or the "reciprocity" reservation.

As indicated on page 123, under the "reciprocity reservation" the state in which enforcement is being sought has formally stated that it will apply the Convention to the recognition or enforcement of awards made only in the territory of a contracting state to the Convention. This overrides the general rule that a state where the arbitral award is made does not normally have to be a party to the New York Convention in order for an application for recognition and/or enforcement of that award to be made in another state pursuant to that Convention. (A list of the states availing themselves of this reservation may be found in Appendix 1, column 1.)

As indicated on page 5 above, under the "commercial reservation" the state in which enforcement is being sought has formally stated that it will only permit recognition and/or enforcement of awards under the Convention in respect of differences arising out of legal relationships which are regarded as commercial under the law of that state, notwithstanding the fact that the state in which the award was made is a party to the Convention. (See Appendix 1, column 2, for the identity of those states availing themselves of this reservation.)

The ability to use the commercial reservation in particular to defeat an application will be relatively rare in international commercial arbitration. However, both reservations should be taken into account when the parties are choosing the seat of the arbitration, and considering when they may need to enforce an award.

SECURITY PENDING THE OUTCOME OF A CHALLENGE

Once an arbitral award has been issued, there is normally no reason why the successful party cannot proceed immediately with an application to have it enforced even if the unsuccessful party has lodged an application to set aside. The law of the state in which the application for enforcement is made may, however, permit a stay of the enforcement proceedings pending the outcome of the application to set aside. The stay may be made subject to the condition that the applicant gives security for the amount of the award (for example, under Article VI of the New York Convention).

STATE IMMUNITY

State immunity is not so much a defence as an obstacle to the enforcement of an award against a state. More precisely, it prevents the enforcement of an arbitral award against the assets of the state or state agency. In every case, the law of the state in which enforcement is sought must be considered to establish the extent to which it is an obstacle. The law of some states provides the foreign state with absolute immunity from enforcement against its property, whereas the law of other states does, for example, permit enforcement against the commercial assets of a state.

Where the successful party has had sufficient foresight, it will have attempted to include in the arbitration agreement a waiver of the state's immunity from execution (see page 37 above). The effect of such a waiver should nevertheless be carefully checked under the law of the state in which enforcement is sought.

THE CONSEQUENCES OF SUCCESSFULLY RESISTING AN APPLICATION FOR THE RECOGNITION AND/OR ENFORCEMENT OF A FOREIGN AWARD

A party which has successfully resisted an application for recognition and/or enforcement might think that that is the end of the matter. However, that may not be correct if there are assets in any other state. Such a party should bear in mind the following points:

(a) The decision of the state court refusing the application for recognition or enforcement does not have the effect of setting aside or otherwise invalidating the award. The award remains valid and, even though it may not be recognised or enforced in the country in which the application has been refused, it remains possible (subject to the defences which may be established in the relevant court) that the award will be recognised and/or enforced in another jurisdiction where assets may be located.

(b) The decision of the court refusing the application for recognition and/or enforcement is not binding on the courts of any other jurisdiction in which such an application may be made.

(c) Where successful resistance was based on a "public policy" defence under Article V(2) of the New York Convention (see page 132 above), that defence may not be available in other jurisdictions. (Note that there is some support for introducing a standardised set of internationally recognised public policy defences to enforcement, but at the time of writing no such global standard has been adopted.)

CHAPTER 11

INVESTMENT TREATY ARBITRATION

INTRODUCTION

Historically, investors whose investments were confiscated or damaged by the authorities of the state in which they had invested ("the Host State") had few rights of redress. Private individuals and corporations have no standing in international law to bring a claim against a state. Wronged investors had only two options. They could attempt to enforce their contractual right (if any) in the state courts of the Host State. Alternatively, they could appeal to their own state to put pressure on the Host State or to take legal action in an international forum, on the investor's behalf. Neither was a satisfactory remedy. However, the last 50 years have seen a major change, as the international community has taken action to create direct rights and effective remedies for investors.

Investors with disputes involving the governments of states in which they have invested are likely to encounter many of the same difficulties as investors with private disputes. There are, however, a number of issues particular to the field of investor-state dispute resolution that merit separate mention. This chapter provides an overview of the evolving field of international investment treaty arbitration, describing the key developments, most notably the Convention on the Settlement of Investment Disputes between States and Nationals of Other States of 1965 and the establishment of the International Centre for the Settlement of Investment Disputes (ICSID), the growth in the number of bilateral (and some multilateral) investment treaties, the nature of the rights commonly provided by investment treaties, and the features of arbitration conducted under the auspices of ICSID.

THE ICSID CONVENTION

The Convention on the Settlement of Investment Disputes between States and Nationals of Other States (also known as the "ICSID Convention" or the "Washington Convention") was conceived by the Executive Directors of the International Bank for Reconstruction and Development (the World Bank) in 1965. It entered into force in 1966 with 20 member governments acting as signatories. As indicated on page 18, the ICSID Convention established ICSID, one of the five organisations that make up the World Bank Group. The goal of the ICSID Convention is to support and encourage the flow of foreign direct investment into states wishing to attract such investment.

Prior to the ICSID Convention, cross-border investment was hindered by the absence of a neutral and effective mechanism for the resolution of investment disputes between investors and the host state in which they had invested. With the aim of eradicating this obstacle to investor confidence, the ICSID Convention established a mechanism whereby non-state entities – nationals of one party to the Convention – may submit disputes with governments of other states party to the Convention directly to arbitration, under the neutral auspices of the Centre.

The concept proved popular and membership of the Convention grew quickly from the time of its inception. Submission of disputes to the Centre was, however, rare in the early years. While ICSID arbitration clauses became common in large scale government contracts the trend did not extend to foreign investment contracts generally.

BILATERAL AND MULTILATERAL INVESTMENT TREATIES

Subsequent to the signing of the Convention, states began to conclude bilateral investment treaties (BITs) containing "standing offers" to submit disputes arising out of an investment made by a national of the other state party, to ICSID or other binding international arbitration. There are now over 2,000 BITs in existence and over 140 states are party to at least one such treaty. The vast majority of BITs contain "standing offers" or advance consent to arbitrate investment disputes at ICSID or in accordance with arbitration rules such as the UNCITRAL Arbitration Rules. A growing number of BITs also include the option of submitting disputes to other institutions, such as the ICC or the Arbitration Institute of the Stockholm Chamber of Commerce. Some states have also enacted generalised foreign investment promotion and protection laws, which include similar provisions and are applicable to all foreign investors regardless of their nationality.

Investors benefit from this new form of arbitration in a number of ways. Direct recourse to arbitration against the Host State provides greater assurance that investments will be treated fairly. The substantive protections under investment treaties may be more comprehensive than those negotiated under a particular contract or may provide additional safeguards. Rights and protections available under public international law may be enforced without the assistance of one's home government. The ability to initiate proceedings against a state, in the absence of any contractual agreement to do so, increases investors' ability to obtain compensation for acts or omissions by the host state which indirectly harm the value of their investment.

Another development in the field of investment treaty arbitration is the advent of the Multilateral Investment Treaty (MIT). MITs contain protections similar to those found in BITs and invariably provide for resolution of disputes by international arbitration. For example, the Energy Charter Treaty has, at the time of writing, been signed by 52 countries. Existing regional MITs include the 1994 North American Free Trade Agreement, or NAFTA (between Mexico, Canada and the USA); the 1991 Colonia Investment Protocol of the Common Market of the Southern Cone, or Mercosur (between Argentina, Brazil, Paraguay and Uruguay); and the 1994 Cartagena Free Trade Agreement (between Colombia, Mexico and Venezuela). The NAFTA, in particular, has played an important role in the development of investment treaty arbitration. A number of NAFTA cases, which tend to be more highly publicised than other cases, have led to important rulings on the standards of protection under international law. Since its entry into force, several new BITs have been modelled upon the detailed investment provisions of the NAFTA.

Identifying applicable treaties

The table in Appendix 7 lists certain key bilateral investment treaties or laws. Otherwise ICSID's website (*www.worldbank.org/icsid*) or the UNCTAD website (*www.unctad.org*) are the best reference sources to establish quickly whether the particular states in which the investor has an interest have entered into a BIT. There is, however, no comprehensive list of BITs. Consulting the foreign or finance ministry or the embassies of the relevant states is the only definitive way to verify the existence or non-existence of a BIT.

Who is protected?

An investment protection treaty is concluded between states in order to provide protection to nationals of each state. "Nationals" include both natural persons and companies; a company is generally treated as a national of the state in which it is incorporated or registered. Since many states require investments to be channelled through a local company, investment treaties often provide that a company which is incorporated in the Host State, but whose shares are owned by nationals of the Home State, shall be treated as a company of the Home State. It is sometimes possible for an investor to shop around for an applicable treaty, or for the most favourable treaty, by investing through a subsidiary company in a state which has negotiated a treaty with the Host State. However, it is important to note that investment treaties incorporate different tests for the nationality of the investor. For some treaties, the investor's nationality will be that of the state in which the corporation engaged in the investment is incorporated or registered. In others, it is where the seat of management is based.

Investment treaties do not usually define what constitutes "conduct of a Host State". However, it is a recognised tenet of public international law that the conduct of any state organ, whether exercising a judicial, executive or legislative function, is attributable to the state as a whole.

Rights commonly provided by BITs and MITs

This section addresses the legal regime that is created by the treatment provisions of investment treaties and laws. While there are variations in emphasis and formulation/approach from one treaty to another, the majority of BITs and MITs undertake to guarantee the following standards of treatment:

(a) *Fair and equitable treatment*: The standard of treatment which constitutes "fair and equitable treatment" is commonly subject to two interpretations by states and tribunals. One interpretation is that the treatment required need not exceed the minimum standard of treatment of aliens under customary international law. The other interpretation is that the treatment required is that which may only be ascertained by applying the plain meaning of the terms to the specific facts of each individual case. Exclusive of any reference to any established body of law or practice, a state or tribunal must carry out a subjective non-technical assessment of what treatment would be fair and equitable in the circumstances. The consequences of applying one interpretation over the other may be significant, as is borne out by recent case law. In 2001, the NAFTA Free Trade Commission issued an interpretative note on the appropriate interpretation of the fair and equitable treatment in the NAFTA. Drafters of some of the new investment treaties have also begun to supplement or rework the standard formulation of the provision so as to clearly indicate the appropriate interpretation to be applied.

(b) *Full protection and security*: Investment treaties and laws usually provide that investments will be accorded "full protection and security" by the Host State. As with the fair and equitable treatment protection the exact standard of this provision is still ill-defined. Case law, however, indicates that Host States are obliged to exercise "reasonable care" and "due diligence" in protecting investments. The undertaking of full protection and security is often featured alongside the general guarantee of fair and equitable treatment, but in practice the phrase has been interpreted as applying only where the physical protection of the investment is at issue.

(c) *Protection against uncompensated expropriation or nationalisation*: The scope of protection offered under this provision extends not only to the physical or legal expropriation of property, but also to measures which, whilst not depriving an investor of the legal right to property, nonetheless substantially diminish its value or another benefit to be derived from it. Examples would be the revocation of a permit required to operate a business or excessive or arbitrary taxation. An expropriatory taking is lawful if it is:

(i) for a public purpose;

(ii) non discriminatory; and

(iii) subject to prompt, adequate and effective compensation.

(d) *National treatment*: This provision guarantees an investor treatment no less favourable than that which a Host State accords to its own nationals. The standard of treatment owed under this provision is thus relative and contingent upon that accorded to a domestic investor in the Host State. The undertaking of non-discrimination that lay at the core of this protection is also seldom without limitation. Often investment treaties provide that such treatment will apply only "in like circumstances" or "similar situations". It is not uncommon for the provision of national treatment to be restricted to the post-establishment phase of an investment, with many treaties containing a separate admission and establishment clause. Addenda to treaties may include protocols allowing state parties to exempt certain industries from the national treatment obligation.

(e) *"Most favoured nation" treatment*: As implied by its terms, the most favoured nation ("MFN") provision requires the Host State to accord to investors of the state who are beneficiary to the clause treatment that is as, or more, favourable than that given to investors of any third state. As with national treatment, the standard of treatment owed is wholly relative and contingent upon that accorded by the Host State to other foreign investors. MFN provisions may contain qualifications similar to those found in national treatment clauses. Taken together, national and MFN treatment provisions create a minimum standard of treatment of covered investors which is equal to the best treatment provided by the Host State to investors of any other nationality.

(f) *Protection against breach of the investment contract*: Treaties commonly provide that the Host State "shall observe any obligation it may have entered into with regard to investments of nationals or companies of the other Contracting Party [Home State]". Such provisions, known as "umbrella clauses" because they cover only specific undertakings with a particular investor, are prevalent in modern BITs, but until recently have attracted little attention. In one ruling, an ICSID tribunal affirmed the significance of the plain meaning of the obligation under the treaty, but stayed its decision on the claim until the parties had pursued the recourse provided under the exclusive jurisdiction provision in their contract.

(g) *Compensation for losses due to war or riot*: Most investment treaties provide that investors suffering losses owing to war, other armed conflict, revolution, state of national emergency, insurrection or riot in the Host State shall receive compensation in accordance with the national treatment or MFN treatment standards (treatment no less favourable than that which is accorded to either its own nationals or to the nationals of any third state).

(h) *Right to transfer and repatriate investments and investment returns*: Nearly all investment treaties contain some provision guaranteeing the right of investors to transfer the investment, and any returns on the investment, into freely convertible currency. These rights may be subject to qualifications or restrictions set out in the provision or expressed in an addendum to the treaty. Restrictions usually relate to timing of the transfer. It is usually provided that limitations may only be made on a non-discriminatory basis.

(i) *Subrogation*: Investment treaty subrogation provisions allow export credit and political risk insurance agencies such as the ECGD, OPIC or EID/MITI to claim directly against the Host State where an indemnity has been paid to the investor.

ACCESS TO INTERNATIONAL ARBITRATION

Many investment treaties and laws provide that disputes relating to investments between foreign investors and a Host State will be referred to independent binding arbitration (often ICSID or UNCITRAL arbitration). Sometimes, the right to submit a dispute to arbitration may arise only after attempts have been made to reach an amicable resolution or to pursue local remedies. This will depend on the wording of the treaty or law. It is generally accepted that, unless otherwise provided, and subject to important public policy considerations, arbitration proceedings can be commenced without exhausting local remedies, although there may still be a required period for negotiations. In one recent case an investor succeeded in bypassing the procedural requirements contained in the BIT between his own state and the Host State on the basis of the application of the MFN provision, which allowed him to avail himself of a more favourable provision, contained in another BIT.

THE CHOICE OF AN ARBITRATION FORUM

Investment treaties typically provide a host of optional mechanisms for resolving disputes. Assuming that the aggrieved investor does not wish to try the dispute in the local courts of the Host State, remaining options normally include a choice between institutional or non-institutional arbitration proceedings. As mentioned above, ICSID is the institutional forum that features most often in investment treaties. The most common form of non-institutional arbitration is under the UNCITRAL Arbitration Rules. Occasionally, reference is made to a domestic arbitral institution.

Of the possible choices of institutional forums, ICSID, if available, is the most favourable choice.

ADVANTAGES OF ICSID ARBITRATION

The advantages of ICSID arbitration include:

(a) *Application of international law*: Unless the parties agree otherwise, ICSID tribunals are charged with applying the law of the Host State party and such rules of international law as are applicable. In practice, this has meant that in order to comply with obligations set out in a treaty, states' conduct must meet the requirements of both domestic and international law.

(b) *Greater insulation from domestic regimes*: Unlike other arbitral institutions ICSID has its own internal procedure for challenging arbitral awards. ICSID awards cannot be challenged in state courts; any request for annulment of the award is determined by another ICSID tribunal set up for that purpose. This means that ICSID proceedings and awards are better protected from interference by state courts.

(c) *Enforceable awards*: ICSID awards are more easily, and more widely, enforceable than arbitral awards which are enforced under the New York Convention. At the time of writing, 140 states have ratified the ICSID Convention. A list of contracting states to the ICSID Convention is set out in Appendix 8. ICSID awards are enforceable in the state courts of all contracting states, as if they were final judgments of the state courts, without any right of challenge. By contrast, as discussed on pages 130–132 above, the New York Convention provides seven separate grounds on which an award may be challenged, including the general ground that the arbitral award is contrary to public policy.

(d) *World Bank support*: ICSID is one of the five institutions (along with the IMF, IFC, MIGA and the IDA) that make up the World Bank Group. Unlike other arbitral proceedings, the registration and progress of ICSID proceedings are matters of public record. There is a belief that non-compliance with an ICSID arbitral award by a contracting state may result in that state being unable to obtain loans and credits from other Bank institutions in the future. This can have the effect of persuading parties to comply with awards and even to settle unmeritorious cases rather than risk their relationship with the Bank.

(e) *Extensive administrative support*: Administrative support is provided by the legal staff of the Secretariat of ICSID. Each tribunal is assigned its own secretary. Functions of the secretary of the tribunal include serving as a channel of communications between parties and arbitrators, arranging meetings, keeping minutes, preparing drafts of procedural orders, processing payments of claims of the arbitrators and claims for other expenditure incurred by the proceeding, and providing such other assistance to all parties as may be needed in connection with the proceedings.

(f) *Prohibition of diplomatic protection*: An advantage for Host States is that the ICSID Convention prohibits the intervention of the investor's Home State in the dispute by way of diplomatic protection or the making of an international claim against the Host State (on behalf of the investor) unless the Host State has failed to comply with an ICSID award (Article 27(1)).

WHEN IS ICSID ARBITRATION AVAILABLE?

The ICSID Convention itself does not confer rights on the investor. It simply makes the ICSID mechanism available where an investor has a dispute with a contracting state or state entity which has provided, or is prepared to provide, its consent to ICSID arbitration. Broadly speaking, an investor will only have the right to request ICSID arbitration if there is an ICSID arbitration clause in his contract with a state or state entity, if there is an applicable BIT, MIT or foreign investment law in which the state has given its advance consent to ICSID arbitration, or if both the Host State and the Home State of the investor are contracting states to the ICSID Convention and the Host State is prepared to grant its contemporaneous consent.

ICSID's jurisdiction extends to "any legal dispute arising directly out of an investment, between a contracting state (or any constituent subdivision or agency of a contracting state designated to the Centre by that state) and a national of another contracting state, which the parties to the dispute consent in writing to submit to the Centre" (Article 25(1)). ICSID will also administer certain other arbitrations under the Additional Facility Rules, but the provisions of the Convention do not apply to those arbitrations (the Additional Facility is described in more detail below).

Arbitration procedure

The ICSID Arbitration Rules cover the areas normally covered by most international arbitration rules. As is generally the case, the constitution and experience of the arbitral tribunal will be a critical factor in determining the efficiency and suitability of the procedure adopted in a particular case.

Registration of the request for arbitration

Arbitration proceedings are initiated by the claimant with the submission of a Request for Arbitration along with the applicable fee. Until quite recently, it was possible to request that the secretariat review a draft of the Request for

Arbitration before its formal submission (to allow the claimant to address any blatant jurisdictional problems) but this practice has been discontinued. The Secretary-General of ICSID is charged with the duty of the initial screening of formal Requests for Arbitration. Upon receiving a Request, the Secretary-General must decide, on the basis of information contained in the Request, whether the dispute falls manifestly outside the jurisdiction of the Centre. The response of the respondent state, positive, negative or at all, is not a pre-condition to registration of the Request. It is not uncommon, however, for ICSID to request verification of formal documents and other essential assertions prior to registering the Request.

Constitution of the tribunal

The constitution of the tribunal takes place as soon as possible after the registration of the Request. The parties may choose any uneven number of arbitrators to hear the dispute and are free to agree on the method of appointment. If the parties are unable to agree on the number of arbitrators or the method of their appointment, the ICSID rules provide that the tribunal shall consist of three arbitrators, one appointed by each party and a third to preside as President of the tribunal, to be appointed by agreement of the parties. If the parties fail to agree, or should any party fail to appoint an arbitrator within 90 days of the registration of the Request or such period as the parties have agreed, the Secretary-General of ICSID will, in consultation with the parties, appoint the remaining arbitrators.

The tribunal must hold its first hearing within 60 days of the date of its constitution or within such period as the parties have agreed. At the first hearing, after consulting with the Secretary-General and parties, the tribunal sets the dates of the subsequent hearings and the manner and schedule of the pleadings.

Although the ICSID rules provide that the arbitration will be held at the seat of the Centre (Washington DC), the Centre has concluded special arrangements with seven other arbitral institutions where the proceedings may be held if the parties so desire. These are: the Permanent Court of Arbitration in The Hague, the two Regional Arbitration Centres of the Asian-African Legal Consultative Committee in Cairo and Kuala Lumpur, the Australian Centre for International Commercial Arbitration in Melbourne, the Australian Commercial Disputes Centre in Sydney, the Singapore International Arbitration Centre and the Gulf Cooperation Council Commercial Arbitration Centre in Bahrain. Proceedings may be held elsewhere if the parties agree, subject to certain conditions. It is not uncommon for ICSID tribunals to take advantage of modern communications technology by holding meetings of the tribunal and session with the parties by telephone conference or video-link (see the section on the use of information technology in arbitration on pages 106–108 above). In total, about half of all arbitration proceedings brought under the ICSID Convention are held in Washington DC.

Procedural languages

The official procedural languages are English, French and Spanish. Parties may freely agree on the use of one or two of these languages in the proceedings. If they do not agree on a single procedural language, each party may select one of the official languages for this purpose. If two languages are selected, the orders and award of the tribunal will be rendered and the record of the proceedings kept in both languages.

Costs and duration of proceedings

ICSID's administrative expenditure, including the remuneration of its Secretariat, is covered by the World Bank, except for (at the time of writing) a US$15,000 lodging fee when a request for arbitration is lodged and a US$5,000 administrative fee following the constitution of the tribunal. ICSID does not charge for the use of hearing rooms at its Washington DC headquarters.

Apart from this, the costs of ICSID arbitration depend upon its duration. The average length of time between registration of a claim and rendition of an award on the merits is about 2½ years. In one case that was settled amicably 6 months after the constitution of the tribunal, the arbitrators' costs came to only US$3,000. At the other end of the spectrum, in proceedings that lasted over 7 years, direct costs totalled over US$760,000. The Centre will request refundable advance payments from the parties in respect of the direct costs based on an estimate of their likely amount.

Article 61 of the ICSID Convention provides that the tribunal will determine in its award how and by whom the administrative fees, the direct costs and the parties' legal fees shall ultimately be borne. In the majority of cases, fees and expenses of the arbitrators and the Centre's fees are split equally between the parties and legal costs are left to be borne by the party which incurred them. Some investment treaties stipulate that the parties will bear their own costs. Where the decision is left to the discretion of the tribunal, factors such as the manner in which a party has conducted itself and how successful a party has been may influence the tribunal's ruling.

ENFORCEMENT OF ICSID AWARDS

The ICSID Convention provides that a party to an ICSID award may obtain recognition and enforcement by furnishing a copy of the award, certified by the ICSID Secretary-General, to a competent court of a contracting state. Recognition and enforcement under the Convention is only available in a state that is a signatory to, and which has ratified, the Convention. There is no provision for challenge to an award in the state courts of a contracting state (by contrast to the regime under the New York Convention, as noted above). Article 53 of the ICSID Convention states that an ICSID award shall not be subject to any appeal or remedy other than those provided for in the Convention. Article 54 requires contracting states to enforce the pecuniary obligations imposed by the award within its territories, as if it were a final judgment of a court in that state. In England, special provisions for the enforcement of ICSID awards are set out in the Arbitration (International Investment Disputes) Act 1966. There will normally be similar legislation in other countries which have ratified the Convention.

The ICSID Convention provides for four post-award remedies. After an award has been rendered, either of the parties may request rectification (whereby omissions to decide a question or typographical and arithmetical errors may be corrected), interpretation, revision (on discovery of previously unknown facts) or annulment (where the tribunal was improperly constituted, manifestly exceeded its powers, departed from a fundamental rule of proce-dure, failed to state its reasons, or was corrupt) under Articles 49 to 52. Such requests are dealt with by the original tribunal where feasible or (in the case of the annulment procedure) by a specially appointed *ad hoc* committee. Concerns have been voiced in the past over the use of the annulment proce-dure (Article 52) by which awards have been set aside in three cases to date, leaving the parties to start fresh arbitration proceedings or otherwise settle their dispute. However, early fears about unjustified use of the procedure appear from recent experience to have been unfounded.

Probably because ICSID proceedings are supported by the World Bank, there has been only one instance of a state refusing to comply with an ICSID award. Breach of the ICSID Convention through non-compliance with an ICSID award restores the right of the contracting state, whose national is the award creditor, to give diplomatic protection to its national and to bring an international claim on its behalf.

ICSID ADDITIONAL FACILITY ARBITRATION

In 1978, ICSID adopted the Additional Facility Rules which provide access to ICSID administered arbitration in certain situations where the Con-vention's jurisdictional requirements are not met. The Additional Facility can be used for:

(a) arbitration proceedings for the settlement of investment disputes aris-ing between parties, one of which is not a contracting state or a nation-al of a contracting state; and

(b) arbitration proceedings between parties, at least one of which is a con-tracting state or a national of a contracting state for the settlement of disputes that do not directly arise out of an investment.

The terms on which the Secretariat may administer these proceedings are set out in the Additional Facility Rules. They provide, among other things, that the Additional Facility is only available for the settlement of investment disputes and not ordinary commercial disputes, and that parties must seek the approval of the Secretary-General of ICSID in order to institute proceedings. The Additional Facility is used most often to administer arbitrations arising out of BITs or investment laws where either the Host State or the Home State of the investor is not a party to the ICSID Convention. The first cases under the Additional Facility were registered in 1997.

It is important to note that, although ICSID will administer arbitration proceedings brought under the Additional Facility, the Convention is not applicable to the proceedings. Consequently, the arbitration proceedings are not insulated from state laws and recognition and enforcement of any award is governed by the law of the relevant state and any applicable conventions, such as the New York Convention. For these reasons, the Additional Facility Rules provide that such proceedings may only be held in countries which are parties to the New York Convention (Article XIX). The special procedures which apply to applications for the annulment of ICSID arbitration awards do not apply to Additional Facility arbitration awards.

CHALLENGES TO JURISDICTION

In nearly all of the cases brought before ICSID, the respondent state has challenged the jurisdiction of the tribunal. The contentions on which such challenges are founded are commonly:

(a) that the dispute involves potential liability on the part of the state. Sometimes, states will contend that the dispute is with the company or agency with whom the investor has contracted, which may be a public or administrative body separate from the state itself;

(b) that the claimant has failed to exhaust local or other remedies where there was an obligation to do so;

(c) that there is no "investment" within the meaning of the Convention; and

(d) that the state has not given consent to arbitration.

Careful consideration should be given to anticipating possible jurisdictional objections when preparing a case for filing at ICSID.

PRACTICAL CONSIDERATIONS

Any individual or corporation engaged in commercial activity outside its Home State should always consider whether the ICSID Convention or an investment treaty or foreign investment law could apply. The following is a summary of some of the important matters to be considered when contracting and/or when problems arise.

Making a preliminary determination

(a) Are the Home and/or Host states parties to the ICSID Convention and have they ratified the Convention?

(b) Does the Host State have a foreign investment law? Are the Home and Host States parties to an investment treaty?

(c) Does the commercial activity come within the definition of investment given in an applicable investment treaty or law?

Matters which should be considered when contracting

Assuming that the answers to the previous questions suggest that the ICSID Convention or an investment treaty or foreign investment law might apply:

(a) Are you contracting with a state which is party to the ICSID Convention? Is the prospective investor from a state party to the Convention or is the investment incorporated in a state which is party to the Convention? If so, consider incorporating an ICSID arbitration clause into the contract.

(b) Consider whether the ICSID arbitration clause should cover any other optional matters which are permitted within the ICSID arbitration regime, such as waiver of immunity from execution of the award, provision of procedures for nominating the arbitrators, selection of the place of proceedings and determination of the division of costs. ICSID has helpfully provided suggested wording to cover these and other matters. The text of these clauses can be found on the ICSID website (*www.worldbank.org/icsid/model-clauses – en/main.htm*).

(c) It is advisable to negotiate a clause which permits applications to local or other courts for interim measures prior to constitution of an ICSID tribunal. This allows one party to attempt, for example, to restrain the other from disposing of evidence or funds prior to the tribunal hearing, or to apply for an injunction against the enforcement of regulations which adversely affect the interests in dispute.

(d) Is there an applicable BIT, MIT or foreign investment law?

  (i) If the Home State of the investor is not a party to an investment treaty, consider whether a corporate vehicle incorporated in a state which is party to such a treaty could be the investor.

  (ii) If it is uncertain whether your commercial activity qualifies as an investment, consider the way the activity is described in the contract. Changes to the description may make clear that the activity amounts to an investment and a record that it was the parties' intention to treat the transaction as an investment will be persuasive evidence before a tribunal.

  (iii) Consider the nature of the protection provided by the applicable investment treaty or law. Provisions such as a Most Favoured Nation clause will strengthen your negotiating position later.

(iv) Check the dispute resolution procedures in the investment treaty or law. If it is a foreign investment law, does it provide recourse to an independent arbitration forum? Is there a requirement to exhaust local remedies? Consider whether the dispute resolution provision in the contract is consistent with the investment treaty. You may want to mirror the dispute resolution provision found in the investment treaty or law.

Matters which should be considered if problems arise

(a) If there is an investment treaty or foreign investment law, establish the extent of the protection offered by the treaty or law. This may be greater than immediately apparent from the text. The rights provided by the investment treaty or law may strengthen your negotiating position with the Host State. For example, if the treaty includes a Most Favoured Nation provision, it will be necessary to consider the provisions of other investment treaties entered into by the Host State. Similarly, a provision which guarantees equal protection to that given to nationals of the Host State would require an analysis of treatment accorded to domestic investors.

(b) Remember, it is not necessary to have entered into a contract with a state entity in order to avail oneself of the protections provided under a BIT or MIT.

(c) Check the dispute resolution procedure in both the contract and the investment treaty or law and make sure that any specific requirements or pre-conditions are satisfied. Investment treaties commonly provide that there should be a period of negotiation prior to the commencement of proceedings and many require notice of intent to claim under the treaty. Keep a good record of documentation relating to these efforts.

(d) Be aware that, as noted above, challenges to the jurisdiction of the ICSID arbitral tribunal are commonly raised by way of defence. The manner in which the dispute develops and is articulated in correspondence or negotiations may pre-empt some jurisdictional challenges. Correspondence may be helpful in establishing that the state refused to take any steps to protect the investment from harm. Similarly, it may be helpful in illuminating the link between an apparently non-governmental entity and the state.

STATES IN WHICH THE NEW YORK CONVENTION OF 1958 HAS ENTERED INTO FORCE (AS AT 1 JANUARY 2004)

The states in which the New York Convention has entered into force are set out in the table below. A number of such states have done so subject to one or both of the reservations permitted by Article I of the New York Convention:

(a) The states taking advantage of the "reciprocity" reservation are indicated in column 1. Each such state will apply the Convention to the recognition and enforcement of awards made only in the territory of the state which is a contracting state to the Convention.

(b) The states taking advantage of the "commercial" reservation are indicated in column 2. Each such state will apply the Convention only to differences arising out of legal relationships, whether contractual or not, which are regarded as commercial under the law of such state.

There are additional notes made in relation to certain other factors which are specific to some states.

State	Column 1 Reciprocity Reservation	Column 2 Commercial Reservation	Notes
Albania			
Algeria	*	*	
Antigua and Barbuda			
Argentina	*	*	1
Armenia	*	*	
Australia			
Austria			
Azerbaïjan			
Bahrain	*	*	
Bangladesh			
Barbados	*	*	
Belarus			2
Belgium	*		
Benin			
Bolivia			
Bosnia and Herzegovina	*	*	3
Botswana	*	*	
Brazil			
Brunei Darussalam	*		
Bulgaria	*		2
Burkina Faso			
Cambodia			
Cameroon			

State	Column 1 Reciprocity Reservation	Column 2 Commercial Reservation	Notes
Canada		★	4
Central African Republic	★	★	
Chile			
China	★	★	
Colombia			
Costa Rica			
Côte d'Ivoire			
Croatia	★	★	3
Cuba	★	★	2
Cyprus	★	★	
Czech Republic			
Denmark	★	★	
Djibouti			
Dominica			
Dominican Republic			
Ecuador	★	★	
Egypt, Arab Rep. of			
El Salvador			
Estonia			
Finland			
France	★		
Georgia			
Germany			
Ghana			
Greece	★	★	
Guatemala			
Guinea			
Haiti			
Holy See (Vatican)	★	★	
Honduras			
Hungary	★	★	
Iceland			
India	★	★	
Indonesia	★	★	
Iran, Islamic Rep. of	★	★	
Ireland	★		
Israel			
Italy			
Jamaica	★	★	
Japan	★		
Jordan			
Kazakhstan			
Kenya	★		
Korea, Rep. of	★	★	
Kuwait	★		
Kyrgyzstan			
Lao People's Democratic Rep.			
Latvia			
Lebanon	★		
Lesotho			
Lithuania			2

State	Column 1 Reciprocity Reservation	Column 2 Commercial Reservation	Notes
Luxembourg	★		
Macedonia, former Yugoslav Rep. of			
Madagascar	★	★	
Malaysia	★	★	
Mali			
Malta	★		5
Mauritania			
Mauritius	★		
Mexico			
Moldova, Rep. of	★		3
Monaco	★	★	
Mongolia	★	★	
Morocco	★		
Mozambique	★		
Nepal	★	★	
Netherlands	★		
New Zealand	★		
Nicaragua			
Niger			
Nigeria	★	★	
Norway	★		6
Oman			
Panama			
Paraguay			
Peru			
Philippines	★	★	
Poland	★	★	
Portugal	★		
Qatar			
Romania	★	★	2
Russian Federation			2
Saint Vincent and the Grenadines	★	★	
San Marino			
Saudi Arabia	★		
Senegal			
Serbia and Montenegro	★	★	3
Singapore	★		
Slovak Republic			
Slovenia	★	★	3
South Africa			
Spain			
Sri Lanka			
Sweden			
Switzerland			
Syrian Arab Republic			
Tanzania	★		
Thailand			
Trinidad and Tobago	★	★	
Tunisia	★	★	
Turkey	★	★	

State	Column 1 Reciprocity Reservation	Column 2 Commercial Reservation	Notes
Uganda	★		
Ukraine			2
United Kingdom of Great Britain and Northern Ireland	★		
United States of America	★	★	
Uruguay			
Uzbekistan			
Venezuela			
Vietnam	★	★	2, 7
Zambia			
Zimbabwe			

NOTES:

(These notes do not include territorial declarations and reservations and declarations of a political nature.)

1. Argentina has declared that the Convention should be construed in accordance with the principles and rules of its National Constitution or with those resulting from reforms mandated by the Constitution.

2. In relation to awards made in the territory of states which are not signatories to the Convention, this state will only apply the Convention to the extent to which the state in question grants reciprocal treatment.

3. The Convention will apply only to those arbitral awards which were adopted after the Convention came into effect.

4. The commercial reservation does not apply in the Province of Quebec.

5. The Convention only applies to Malta in respect of arbitration agreements concluded after the date of Malta's accession to the Convention (20 September 2000).

6. The Convention will not be applied in this state where the subject matter of the proceedings is immovable property situated in the state, or a right in or to such property.

7. Vietnam declared that the interpretation of the Convention before the Vietnamese Courts or competent authorities should be made in accordance with the Constitution and the law of Vietnam.

STATES WHICH HAVE BASED THEIR ARBITRATION LAWS ON THE UNCITRAL MODEL LAW

Australia
Azerbaijan
Bahrain
Belarus
Bermuda
Bulgaria
Canada
Croatia
Cyprus
Egypt
Germany
Greece
Guatemala
Hong Kong
Hungary
India
Iran (Islamic Republic of)
Ireland (Republic of)
Japan
Jordan
Kenya

Lithuania
Macau
Madagascar
Malta
Mexico
New Zealand
Nigeria
Oman
Paraguay
Peru
Republic of Korea
Russian Federation
Scotland
Singapore
Spain
Sri Lanka
Thailand
Tunisia
Ukraine
Zambia
Zimbabwe

Independent jurisdictions, within the United States of America, which have based their arbitration laws on the Model Law include:

California
Connecticut
Illinois
Oregon
Texas

COMPARATIVE TABLE OF INTERNATIONAL ARBITRATION RULES

Aspect of arbitration	Institutional arbitration								Ad hoc	
	AAA/ICDR	Rule	ICC	Rule	LCIA	Rule	UNCITRAL	Rule		
Manner in which the arbitration may be commenced	By notice sent to the other party, and the AAA/ICDR.	2(1)	By request sent to Secretariat of the ICC Court, which then notifies the other party.	4(1)	By request sent to the LCIA, with a copy to the other party.	1(1)	By notice sent to the other party	3		
Arbitrators (a) Number of arbitrators who will be appointed	Absent agreement between the parties, 1, unless the AAA/ICDR is of the view that 3 are appropriate.	5	Absent agreement between the parties, 1, unless the ICC Court is of the view that 3 are appropriate.	8(2)	Absent agreement between the parties, 1, unless the LCIA is of the view that 3 are appropriate.	5(4)	Absent agreement between the parties, 3.	5		
(b) Who appoints the arbitrators?	The parties may mutually agree upon any procedure for appointing arbitrators, failing which the AAA/ICDR appoint the arbitrators.	6	The parties may agree a nomination (to be confirmed in any event by the ICC Court), failing which it is by the ICC Court.	8(3) 8(4)	The LCIA, paying regard to methods or criteria of selection agreed by parties.	5(5)	The parties, by agreement or nomination. Failing which it is by the appointing authority designated by the parties. Failing that, by the appointing authority designated by the Secretary-General of the Permanent Court of	7		

	AAA/ICDR	ICC	LCIA	Arbitration, The Hague.
(c) Restrictions on nationality of arbitrators	6(4) No.	9(5) Yes. A sole arbitrator or chairman is not usually to be of the same nationality as a party.	6(1) Yes. A sole arbitrator or chairman is not usually to be of the same nationality as a party.	6(4) Same nationality as one of the parties is permitted, but discouraged.
(d) Time limit for challenge to an arbitrator	8(1) 15 days from the date of notification of his appointment, or becoming aware of the relevant circumstances.	11(2) 30 days from the date of notification of his appointment, or becoming aware of the relevant circumstances.	10(4) 15 days from the date of formation of the arbitral tribunal, or becoming aware of the relevant circumstances.	11(1) 15 days from the date of notification of his appointment, or becoming aware of the relevant circumstances.
Multi-party disputes	6(5) The AAA/ICDR appoints the tribunal, unless the parties have agreed otherwise within 45 days of the commencement of the arbitration.	10 ICC Court appoints tribunal, unless all parties have previously made a joint nomination.	8 LCIA Court appoints tribunal.	No provision.
Seat of the arbitration	13(1) Absent agreement between the parties, this will be determined initially by the AAA/ICDR, with the tribunal having the final say.	14(1) Absent agreement between the parties, this will be determined by the ICC Court.	16(1) Absent agreement between the parties, London, unless the LCIA Court decides otherwise.	16(1) Absent agreement between the parties, the decision is for the tribunal.
Challenges to the jurisdiction of the tribunal	15(1) Made to the tribunal itself.	6(2) The ICC Court will rule on the *prima facie*	23(1) Made to the tribunal itself	21 Made to the tribunal itself.

Aspect of arbitration	Institutional arbitration						Ad hoc	
	AAA/ICDR	Rule	ICC	Rule	LCIA	Rule	UNCITRAL	Rule
			validity of agreement to arbitrate. Other questions of jurisdiction are for the tribunal to decide.	6(2)				
Procedure	Subject to the rules, the tribunal has a discretion in how to conduct the proceedings.	16(1)	The parties may supplement rules in their arbitration agreement. Subject to the rules, the tribunal has a discretion as to how to conduct the proceedings.	15	The parties are encouraged to agree procedures. Any gaps are to be filled by the tribunal.	14	The parties may modify the rules in their arbitration agreement. Subject to the rules, the tribunal has a discretion in how to conduct the proceedings.	1(1) 15(1)
Are proceedings confidential?	Yes.	34	No specific provision, though tribunal may take measures to protect confidential information.	20(7)	Yes.	30	No provision.	
Award (a) Time limit for making the award	None, though the rules state that awards shall be made promptly.	27(1)	6 months from signature of the terms of reference-extendable.	24	None.		None.	
(b) Where there is failure by arbitrators to agree on the award, it may be made	By a majority of the arbitrators.	26(1)	By a majority of the arbitrators, but absent a majority, the Chairman may make the award alone.	25(1)	By a majority of the arbitrators, but absent a majority, the Chairman may make the award alone.	26(3)	By a majority of the arbitrators.	31(1)

(c) Is there scrutiny of award by any other body?	No, but if the arbitration laws of the country where the award is made require the award to be filed or registered, the tribunal shall comply with such requirements. [27(6)]	Yes – by the ICC Court. [27]	No.	No.
Costs:				
(a) Is there an administration fee, and how is it calculated?	Yes – *ad valorem*.	Yes – ad valorem, but with a cap of US$88,800.	Yes – fixed registration fee, time-based administration fee and sum equivalent to 5% of the tribunal's fees for overheads.	No.
(b) How are arbitrators' fees calculated?	By reference to the time expended, their rates, and the size and complexity of the case. [32]	By reference to time expended and the value of the dispute. [31(1); 31(2) Appx III Art.2(2)]	By reference to time, and rates appropriate to the particular circumstances of the case, including its complexity and the special qualifications of the arbitrators.	By reference to time expended, the value of the dispute, the complexity of the subject matter and any other relevant circumstances. If appointing authority is involved, its schedules of fees must be taken into account. [39(1)]
(c) Will the successful party be awarded legal costs?	Yes – at the discretion of the tribunal. [31]	Yes – unless the parties agree otherwise in writing. [31(3)]	Yes – at the discretion of the tribunal. [28(3)]	Yes – at the discretion of the tribunal. [40(2)]
(d) Are deposits required as advance on costs?	Yes – at the discretion of the AAA/ICDR and/or the tribunal. [33]	Yes. [Appx III Art.1]	Yes – at the discretion of the LCIA. [24]	Yes – at the discretion of the tribunal. [41]

Aspect of arbitration	Institutional arbitration						Ad hoc	
	AAA/ICDR	Rule	ICC	Rule	LCIA	Rule	UNCITRAL	Rule
(e) Will security for the costs of the respondent be ordered?	No.		No.		Yes – at the discretion of the tribunal.	25(2)	No.	
Level of institutional administration (see page 31 above)	Fully administered.		Fully administered.		Fully administered, unless the arbitral tribunal directs otherwise.	13(2)	(Not applicable)	
Other relevant aspects			Terms of reference must be drawn up.	18	Awards are final and binding: parties waive right to appeal, insofar as such waiver can validly be made.	26(9)	The rules may be used along with a suitably amended institutional agreement, such as that for the LCIA or ICC.	

STANDARD ARBITRATION CLAUSES RECOMMENDED BY THE AAA/ICDR, THE ICC AND THE LCIA

American Arbitration Association/International Centre for Dispute Resolution

"Any controversy or claim arising out of or relating to this contract, or the breach thereof, shall be determined by arbitration administered by the International Centre for Dispute Resolution in accordance with its International Arbitration Rules."

OR

"Any controversy or claim arising out of or relating to this contract, or the breach thereof shall be determined by the American Arbitration Association in accordance with its International Arbitration Rules."

The parties may wish to consider adding:
    (a) "the number of arbitrators shall be (one or three)";
    (b) "the place of arbitration shall be (city and/or country)"; or
    (c) "the language(s) of the arbitration shall be (specify)".

International Chamber of Commerce

"All disputes arising out of or in connection with the present contract shall be finally settled under the Rules of Arbitration of the International Chamber of Commerce by [one or more]* arbitrator[s] appointed in accordance with the said Rules."

NOTE:
    * Where possible, specify the number of arbitrators. Parties may wish to consider adding directions as to the place and language of the arbitration proceedings, and as to the governing law.

LCIA

"Any dispute arising out of or in connection with this contract, including any question regarding its existence, validity or termination, shall be referred to and finally resolved by arbitration under the LCIA Rules, which Rules are deemed to be incorporated by reference into this clause.

    (i)   The number of arbitrators shall be ... (one or three)
    (ii) The seat, or legal place, of arbitration shall be ... (City and/or Country)
    (iii) The language to be used in the arbitral proceedings shall be ...
    (iv) The governing law of the contract shall be the substantive law of ... "

UNCITRAL MODEL ARBITRATION CLAUSE

"Any dispute, controversy or claim arising out of or relating to this contract, or the breach, termination or invalidity thereof, shall be settled by arbitration in accordance with the UNCITRAL Arbitration Rules as at present in force."

Note: UNCITRAL points out that the parties may wish to consider adding:

"(a) The appointing authority shall be ... (name of institution or person);
(b) The number of arbitrators shall be ... (one or three);
(c) The place of arbitration shall be ... (town or country);
(d) The language(s) to be used in the arbitral proceedings shall be ...".

Parties may also wish to consider modifying the effect of Article 31.1 (which provides for majority decisions, and which could be the cause of delay in the publication of the arbitrators' award) by adding:

"(e) When there are three arbitrators, any award or other decision of the arbitral tribunal shall be made by a majority of the arbitrators. Failing a majority, the award or decision shall be made by the Chairman of the arbitral tribunal alone."

DRAFT NON-INSTITUTIONAL
ARBITRATION CLAUSE
(for arbitrations with three arbitrators)

[NB Headings are included in this appendix simply to assist with the identification of the relevant parts of the clause. They should not be included in the actual arbitration agreement. The headings are cross-referenced to the relevant parts of the main text.]

Submission to arbitration and scope of disputes submitted [page 26]

1. Any dispute, controversy or claim arising out of or relating to this Agreement or its subject matter, including any question regarding its existence, validity or termination, shall be referred to and finally settled by arbitration.

Place and language [pages 27 and 36]

2. The arbitration shall be conducted in [town or country] and in the ... language.

Applicable law [page 35]

3. [The substantive issues between the parties shall be settled in accordance with the laws of ... [country].]*

Appointment and replacement of arbitrators [pages 36 and 65–69]

4. The arbitral tribunal shall comprise three arbitrators who shall be appointed in the following manner:
  (a) Each party shall appoint one arbitrator. The third arbitrator, who shall act as the chairman of the arbitral tribunal, shall be appointed by the party-appointed arbitrators, and written notice of such appointment shall be given to both parties.
  (b) If a party fails to make an appointment of an arbitrator within .... days of receipt of notification of the appointment of an arbitrator by the other party, and/or if the two party-appointed arbitrators fail, within .... days of the appointment of the second arbitrator, to agree upon the appointment of the chairman of the arbitral tribunal, then any such vacancy shall, on the written request of either of the parties, be made by ... [the appointing authority] and both parties notified in writing of such appointment.
  (c) Save as provided for in sub-clause 12 below, if an arbitrator refuses to act, resigns, is incapable of acting, or dies, the vacancy arising shall be supplied in the same manner as that by which such arbitrator was originally appointed.

Procedure [page 91]

5. The arbitral tribunal shall, as soon as possible after it has been constituted, hold a preliminary meeting in order to establish the procedure for the arbitration. Subject

to any mandatory provisions of the laws of ... [place of arbitration] the procedure shall be that which is agreed by the parties or, failing such agreement, that directed by the arbitral tribunal.

Submissions [pages 94 and 97–99]

6. Within ... days of receipt of notice of the appointment of the chairman of the arbitral tribunal, the claimant shall serve on the respondent a statement of case, setting out its claims, and its submissions in support of such claims, together with a copy any documents it intends to rely on.

7. Within ... days of receipt of the claimant's statement of case, the respondent shall serve on the claimant an answer, which shall include any counterclaims, together with a copy of any documents the respondent intends to rely on.

8. The claimant may (and shall do so if the answer includes any counterclaims) within ... days of receipt of the answer, serve on the respondent a reply, together with a copy of any further documents which the claimant intends to rely on.

Equality of treatment [page 85]

9. A copy of any document served by one party on the other shall be sent, at the time of such service, to each of the arbitrators. All communications passing between one party and the arbitral tribunal shall be copied immediately to the other party.

Oral hearing [page 104]

10. Unless the parties agree otherwise in writing, the arbitral tribunal shall hold a hearing at which each party may make oral submissions with regard to the substantive issues.

Party default [pages 84 and 108–109]

11. If either party shall fail to comply with a procedural direction made by the arbitral tribunal, the arbitral tribunal may nevertheless continue with the arbitration and make its award.

The award [pages 74 and 117]

12. Any decision or award of the arbitral tribunal shall, if necessary, be made by a majority. If no majority can be obtained, the chairman shall proceed as if he were a sole arbitrator. If an arbitrator [:

(a) dies, or**
(b)] fails or refuses to take part in the arbitration (and the remaining arbitrators, in their absolute discretion, consider such failure or refusal to be unreasonable),

at any time after the hearing referred to in sub-clause 10 above has commenced, the remaining arbitrators may continue with the arbitration and make an award. In such event, the provisions of sub-clause 4(c) above shall not apply.

Finality [page 113]

13. The award of the arbitral tribunal shall be final and binding upon the parties, and the parties hereby waive their right to any form of appeal insofar as such waiver may validly be made.

Miscellaneous matters [pages 116 and 37]

14. In making its award, the arbitral tribunal shall not have jurisdiction to award punitive damages.***

15. Materials created for the purpose of, and private documents produced by another party in, arbitration proceedings, as well as all awards made in such proceedings, shall be kept confidential, save where a party may be under a legal obligation to make disclosure, or where such disclosure is required to enforce, or make a *bona fide* challenge to, an award.

NOTES:

* This may have been dealt with in the principal agreement.

** A party may not always wish to include this, bearing in mind that it may be its own nominated arbitrator that dies.

*** This is merely one illustration of the kind of provision which may be included in the miscellaneous category. It may be appropriate to include it in an agreement for arbitration in the United States.

LIST OF CERTAIN KEY BILATERAL INVESTMENT TREATIES

The following is a list of the bilateral investment treaties to which China, France, Germany, Italy, The Netherlands, Russia, Spain, the United Kingdom and the United States of America are parties. A full circle (●) indicates a treaty that has been signed and ratified; an open circle (○) indicates a treaty that has been signed. The figure "1" signifies a signed and ratified treaty with Hong Kong and the figure "2" signifies a signed and ratified treaty with Taiwan.

	China	France	Germany	Italy	Netherlands	Russia	Spain	UK	USA
Argentina	●	●	●	●	●	○	●	●	●
Armenia	●	●	○	○				●	●
Australia	●								
Austria	●					●			
Azerbaïjan	●	○	●	○				●	●
Bangladesh	○	●	●	●	●			●	●
Belarus	●	○	●	●	●			●	○
Belgium/Lux.	1								
Bolivia	●	●	●	●	●		●	●	●
Brazil		○	○	○	○			○	
Bulgaria	●	●	●	●	●	○	●	●	●
Chile	●	●	○	●	○		●	●	●
China		●	●	●	●	●	●	●	
Congo		○	●	○				●	●
Congo, Demo. Rep.	○	●	●						●
Costa Rica		○	●		○		○	○	
Croatia	●	●	○	●	●	○	●	●	●
Cuba	○	○	●	●	○	●	●	●	
Czech Rep./ Czechoslovakia	●	●	●	●	●	●	●	●	●
Denmark	●					●			
Ecuador	●	●	●		●	○	●	●	●
Egypt	●	●	●	●	●	○	●	●	●
El Salvador		●	●		●		●		○
Estonia	●	●	●	○	●		●	●	●
Finland	●					●			
Georgia	●	●	●	○	●			●	●
Ghana	●	○	●	○	●			●	
Greece	●		●			●			
Hong Kong, China		●	●	●	●			●	
Hungary	●	●	●	●	●	●	●	●	
India		●	●	●	●	●	●	●	
Indonesia	●	●	●	●	●			●	●
Iran			●	○					
Israel	○	●	○						

	China	France	Germany	Italy	Netherlands	Russia	Spain	UK	USA
Jamaica	●	●	●	●	●			●	●
Japan	1					●			
Jordan		●	●	○	●		○	●	●
Kazakhstan	●	○	●	●			●	●	●
N. Korea						○			
S. Korea	●	●	●	●	●	●	●	●	
Kuwait	●	●	●	●		●			
Latvia	2	●	●	●	●		●	●	●
Lithuania	●	●	●	●	●	○	●	●	○
Malaysia	●	●	●	●	●		●	●	
Mongolia	●	●	●	●	●	○		●	●
Nigeria	○ 2	●			●			●	
Norway	●					●			
Oman	●	●	●	●	●			●	
Pakistan	●	●	●	○	●		●	●	
Panama	2	●	●		●		●	●	●
Paraguay	2	●	●	○	●		●	●	
Peru	●	●	●	●	●		●	●	
Philippines	●	●	○	●	●	○	●	●	
Poland	●	●	●	●	●	○	●	●	●
Portugal	●		●			○			
Romania	●	●	●	●	●	●	●	●	●
Russia	●	●	●	●	●		●	●	○
Saudi Arabia	●		●	●					
Senegal	○	○	●		●			●	●
Singapore	● 2	●	●		●			●	●
South Africa	●	●	●	○	●		○	●	
Sri Lanka	●	●	●	●	●			●	
Sweden	●					●			
Switzerland	●					●			
Tanzania			●		●			●	
Thailand	●		●		●			●	
Tunisia		●	●	●	○		●	●	●
Turkey	●		●	○	●	○	●	●	●
Turkmenistan	●	●	○					●	
Ukraine	●	●	●	●	●	○	○	●	●
UAE	●	●	○	●				●	
Uruguay	●	●	●	●	●		●	●	
Vietnam	●	●	●	●	●	●			
Yemen	○	●	●		●			●	
Yugoslavia	○	●	●		●	●			

LIST OF CONTRACTING STATES AND OTHER SIGNATORIES OF THE WASHINGTON, OR ICSID, CONVENTION (AS OF NOVEMBER 2003)

The 154 states listed below have signed the Washington, or ICSID, Convention on the dates indicated. The names of the 140 States that have deposited their instruments of ratification are in bold, and the dates of such deposit and of the attainment of the status of Contracting State by the entry into force of the Convention for each of them are also indicated.

State	Signature	Deposit of Ratification	Entry into Force of Convention
Afghanistan	30 September 1966	25 June 1968	25 July 1968
Albania	15 October 1991	15 October 1991	14 November 1991
Algeria	17 April 1995	21 February 1996	22 March 1996
Argentina	21 May 1991	19 October 1994	18 November 1994
Armenia	16 September 1992	16 September 1992	16 October 1992
Australia	24 March 1975	2 May 1991	1 June 1991
Austria	17 May 1966	25 May 1971	24 June 1971
Azerbaïjan	18 September 1992	18 September 1992	18 October 1992
Bahamas	19 October 1995	19 October 1995	18 November 1995
Bahrain	22 September 1995	14 February 1996	15 March 1996
Bangladesh	20 November 1979	27 March 1980	26 April 1980
Barbados	13 May 1981	1 November 1983	1 December 1983
Belarus	10 July 1992	10 July 1992	9 August 1992
Belgium	15 December 1965	27 August 1970	26 September 1970
Belize	19 December 1986		
Benin	10 September 1965	6 September 1966	14 October 1966
Bolivia	3 May 1991	23 June 1995	23 July 1995
Bosnia and Herzegovina	25 April 1997	14 May 1997	13 June 1997
Botswana	15 January 1970	15 January 1970	14 February 1970
Brunei Darussalam	16 September 2002	16 September 2002	16 October 2002
Bulgaria	21 March 2000	13 April 2001	13 May 2001
Burkina Faso	16 September 1965	29 August 1966	14 October 1966
Burundi	17 February 1967	5 November 1969	5 December 1969
Cambodia	5 November 1993		
Cameroon	23 September 1965	3 January 1967	2 February 1967
Central African Republic	26 August 1965	23 February 1966	14 October 1966
Chad	12 May 1966	29 August 1966	14 October 1966
Chile	25 January 1991	24 September 1991	24 October 1991
China	9 February 1990	7 January 1993	6 February 1993
Colombia	18 May 1993	15 July 1997	14 August 1997
Comoros	26 September 1978	7 November 1978	7 December 1978
Congo	27 December 1965	23 June 1966	14 October 1966

State	Signature	Deposit of Ratification	Entry into Force of Convention
Congo, Dem. Rep. of	29 October 1968	29 April 1970	29 May 1970
Costa Rica	29 September 1981	27 April 1993	27 May 1993
Côte d'Ivoire	30 June 1965	16 February 1966	14 October 1966
Croatia	16 June 1997	22 September 1998	22 October 1998
Cyprus	9 March 1966	25 November 1966	25 December 1966
Czech Republic	23 March 1993	23 March 1993	22 April 1993
Dominican Rep.	20 March 2000		
Denmark	11 October 1965	24 April 1968	24 May 1968
Ecuador	15 January 1986	15 January 1986	14 February 1986
Egypt, Arab Rep. of	11 February 1972	3 May 1972	2 June 1972
El Salvador	9 June 1982	6 March 1984	5 April 1984
Estonia	23 June 1992	23 June 1992	23 July 1992
Ethiopia	21 September 1965		
Fiji	1 July 1977	11 August 1977	10 September 1977
Finland	14 July 1967	9 January 1969	8 February 1969
France	22 December 1965	21 August 1967	20 September 1967
Gabon	21 September 1965	4 April 1966	14 October 1966
Gambia, The	1 October 1974	27 December 1974	26 January 1975
Georgia	7 August 1992	7 August 1992	6 September 1992
Germany	27 January 1966	18 April 1969	18 May 1969
Ghana	26 November 1965	13 July 1966	14 October 1966
Greece	16 March 1966	21 April 1969	21 May 1969
Grenada	24 May 1991	24 May 1991	23 June 1991
Guatemala	9 November 1995	21 January 2003	20 February 2003
Guinea	27 August 1968	4 November 1968	4 December 1968
Guinea-Bissau	4 September 1991		
Guyana	3 July 1969	11 July 1969	10 August 1969
Haiti	30 January 1985		
Honduras	28 May 1986	14 February 1989	16 March 1989
Hungary	1 October 1986	4 February 1987	6 March 1987
Iceland	25 July 1966	25 July 1966	14 October 1966
Indonesia	16 February 1968	28 September 1968	28 October 1968
Ireland	30 August 1966	7 April 1981	7 May 1981
Israel	16 June 1980	22 June 1983	22 July 1983
Italy	18 November 1965	29 March 1971	28 April 1971
Jamaica	23 June 1965	9 September 1966	14 October 1966
Japan	23 September 1965	17 August 1967	16 September 1967
Jordan	14 July 1972	30 October 1972	29 November 1972
Kazakhstan	23 July 1992	21 September 2000	21 October 2000
Kenya	24 May 1966	3 January 1967	2 February 1967
Kyrgyz, Rep. of	9 June 1995		
Korea, Rep. of	18 April 1966	21 February 1967	23 March 1967
Kuwait	9 February 1978	2 February 1979	4 March 1979
Latvia	8 August 1997	8 August 1997	7 September 1997
Lebanon	26 March 2003	26 March 2003	25 April 2003
Lesotho	19 September 1968	8 July 1969	7 August 1969
Liberia	3 September 1965	16 June 1970	16 July 1970
Lithuania	6 July 1992	6 July 1992	5 August 1992
Luxembourg	28 September 1965	30 July 1970	29 August 1970
Macedonia, former Yugoslav Rep. of	16 September 1998	27 October 1998	26 November 1998

State	Signature	Deposit of Ratification	Entry into Force of Convention
Madagascar	1 June 1966	6 September 1966	14 October 1966
Malawi	9 June 1966	23 August 1966	14 October 1966
Malaysia	22 October 1965	8 August 1966	14 October 1966
Mali	9 April 1976	3 January 1978	2 February 1978
Malta	24 April 2002	3 November 2003	3 December 2003
Mauritania	30 July 1965	11 January 1966	14 October 1966
Mauritius	2 June 1969	2 June 1969	2 July 1969
Micronesia	24 June 1993	24 June 1993	24 July 1993
Moldova	12 August 1992		
Mongolia	14 June 1991	14 June 1991	14 July 1991
Morocco	11 October 1965	11 May 1967	10 June 1967
Mozambique	4 April 1995	7 June 1995	7 July 1995
Namibia	26 October 1998		
Nepal	28 September 1965	7 January 1969	6 February 1969
Netherlands	25 May 1966	14 September 1966	14 October 1966
New Zealand	2 September 1970	2 April 1980	2 May 1980
Nicaragua	4 February 1994	20 March 1995	19 April 1995
Niger	23 August 1965	14 November 1966	14 December 1966
Nigeria	13 July 1965	23 August 1965	14 October 1966
Norway	24 June 1966	16 August 1967	15 September 1967
Oman	5 May 1995	24 July 1995	23 August 1995
Pakistan	6 July 1965	15 September 1966	15 October 1966
Panama	22 November 1995	8 April 1996	8 May 1996
Papua New Guinea	20 October 1978	20 October 1978	19 November 1978
Paraguay	27 July 1981	7 January 1983	6 February 1983
Peru	4 September 1991	9 August 1993	8 September 1993
Philippines	26 September 1978	17 November 1978	17 December 1978
Portugal	4 August 1983	2 July 1984	1 August 1984
Romania	6 September 1974	12 September 1975	12 October 1975
Russian Federation	16 June 1992		
Rwanda	21 April 1978	15 October 1979	14 November 1979
Saint Vincent and the Grenadines	7 August 2001	16 December 2002	15 January 2003
Samoa	3 February 1978	25 April 1978	25 May 1978
Sao Tome and Principe	1 October 1999		
Saudi Arabia	28 September 1979	8 May 1980	7 June 1980
Senegal	26 September 1966	21 April 1967	21 May 1967
Serbia and Montenegro	31 July 2002		
Seychelles	16 February 1978	20 March 1978	19 April 1978
Sierra Leone	27 September 1965	2 August 1966	14 October 1966
Singapore	2 February 1968	14 October 1968	13 November 1968
Slovak Republic	27 September 1993	27 May 1994	26 June 1994
Slovenia	7 March 1994	7 March 1994	6 April 1994
Solomon Islands	12 November 1979	8 September 1981	8 October 1981
Somalia	27 September 1965	29 February 1968	30 March 1968
Spain	21 March 1994	18 August 1994	17 September 1994
Sri Lanka	30 August 1967	12 October 1967	11 November 1967
St Kitts & Nevis	14 October 1994	4 August 1995	3 September 1995
St Lucia	4 June 1984	4 June 1984	4 July 1984
Sudan	15 March 1967	9 April 1973	9 May 1973
Swaziland	3 November 1970	14 June 1971	14 July 1971

State	Signature	Deposit of Ratification	Entry into Force of Convention
Sweden	25 September 1965	29 December 1966	28 January 1967
Switzerland	22 September 1967	15 May 1968	14 June 1968
Tanzania	10 January 1992	18 May 1992	17 June 1992
Thailand	6 December 1985		
Timor-Leste	23 July 2002	23 July 2002	22 August 2002
Togo	24 January 1966	11 August 1967	10 September 1967
Tonga	1 May 1989	21 March 1990	20 April 1990
Trinidad and Tobago	5 October 1966	3 January 1967	2 February 1967
Tunisia	5 May 1965	22 June 1966	14 October 1966
Turkey	24 June 1987	3 March 1989	2 April 1989
Turkmenistan	26 September 1992	26 September 1992	26 October 1992
Uganda	7 June 1966	7 June 1966	14 October 1966
Ukraine	3 April 1998	7 June 2000	7 July 2000
United Arab Emirates	23 December 1981	23 December 1981	22 January 1982
United Kingdom of Gt Britain & N. Ireland	26 May 1965	19 December 1966	18 January 1967
United States of America	27 August 1965	10 June 1966	14 October 1966
Uruguay	28 May 1992	9 August 2000	8 September 2000
Uzbekistan	17 March 1994	26 July 1995	25 August 1995
Venezuela	18 August 1993	2 May 1995	1 June 1995
Yemen, Republic of	28 October 1997		
Zambia	17 June 1970	17 June 1970	17 July 1970
Zimbabwe	25 March 1991	20 May 1994	19 June 1994

SOME USEFUL WEBSITES

American Arbitration Association/International Centre for Dispute Resolution:	*www.adr.org*
Australian Commercial Disputes Centre:	*www.acdcltd.com.au*
Cairo Regional Centre for International Commercial Arbitration:	*www.crcica.org.eg*
Centre for Effective Dispute Resolution:	*www.cedr.co.uk*
Chamber of National and International Arbitration of Milan:	*www.camera-arbitrale.it*
Chartered Institute of Arbitrators:	*www.arbitrators.org*
CIETAC:	*www.cietac.org*
CPR Institute for Dispute Resolution:	*www.cpradr.org*
Deutsche Institution für Schiedsgerichtsbarkeit: (German Arbitration Institute)	*www.dis-arb.de*
Energy Charter Treaty:	*www.encharter.org*
GAFTA:	*www.gafta.com*
Hong Kong International Arbitration Centre:	*www.hkiac.org*
ICC International Court of Arbitration:	*www.iccwbo.org/index_court.asp*
International Arbitration Institute, Paris:	*www.iaiparis.com*
International Bar Association:	*www.ibanet.org*
International Centre for the Settlement of Investment Disputes:	*www.worldbank.org/icsid*
LCIA:	*www.lcia-arbitration.com*
London Maritime Arbitration Association:	*www.lmaa.org.uk*
Lovells International Arbitration Guide:	*www.lovells.com/arbitration*
OHADA:	*www.ohada.com*
Permanent Court of Arbitration:	*www.pca-cpa.org*
Arbitration Institute of the Stockholm Chamber of Commerce:	*www.sccinstitute.com/uk/Home*

Singapore International Arbitration Centre:	*www.siac.org.sg*
Swiss Chambers' Arbitration:	*www.swissarbitration.ch*
UNCTAD's bilateral investment treaty search engine:	*www.unctad.org*
UNCITRAL:	*www.uncitral.org*
UNIDROIT (International Institute for the Unification of Private Law):	*www.unidroit.org*
Venice Court of National and International Arbitration (VENCA):	*www.venca.it*
World Intellectual Property Organisation:	*www.wipo.org*

INDEX

175